QUESTION EVERYTHING
ANCIENT TRUTHS, MODERN SCIENCE

A.G. WALP

Question Everything
Ancient Truths, Modern Science
A.G. Walp, PhD, DMin, EdS

A LETTER FROM THE AUTHOR

I openly admit that I am nobody special. This statement is not a meager attempt at modesty but, instead, to establish the fact that I am just a person who happens to have the audacity to believe that I have the right to question a claim to truth and reality.

In particular, I refer to those who study historical science, e.g., cosmology, geology, paleontology, paleoanthropology, and archeology (as opposed to observational or experimental science that produces modern technology, e.g., computers, bombs, food, et cetera) and proffer their opinion on what history tells us.

I firmly believe that individuals can and should question those who believe they have intellectual authority over them. This is not anarchy, believe it or not; I simply want to verify that the scientific conclusions put forward as factual are reliable. The majority of those who read this book will not have a Ph.D. in said fields, either. I believe, however, that people have the ability to follow a given argument or conclusion to its logical end and determine, to some level, whether the decision of a historical scientist is logical or is wanting.

I do not believe that someone with a superior intellect and more college degrees holds sway to truth and corners the market on what is real, rational, or reliable. I believe that, regardless of my belief system, I have the right to dissect a given person's educated opinions, research, and conclusions. I believe that every person has the right to full disclosure of all available evidence and that I have the right to determine the preponderance of the evidence to direct my cognition of the given data. If someone is blocking variant choices, regardless of how farfetched they may seem to an individual, I want to know what drives him or her to shut the door on my right to have full disclosure.

I am a human with the right to know all that is available, including dissenting opinions, views, and conclusions. When ad hominem assaults begin, it is logical to recognize the personal attack and decipher the attacker's motives. This is important when one considers that personal attacks often indicate a person's lack of knowledge and/or the perceived threat to their worldview, and all that is left to do is address the dissenter's character or intelligence. I, with all due respect, could not care less about a person's worldview when it conflicts with the pursuit of truth. I have great difficulty understanding those who wish to throw insults at those they somehow consider beneath them. I have the right to question their astute observations. Anything less is reminiscent of the Dark Ages, church oppression, and the acts of dozens of other tyrannical authorities throughout the millennia.

If you are in agreement with me, this book is for you. I, like you, am on a journey to glimpse reality, and, regardless of its repercussions, I am an adult who will work through its necessary demands. If you are going to read this book, prepare to set aside preconceived philosophies, personal presuppositions, and prima-donna perceptions. This book unflinchingly examines the clues available to every human. I challenge you to consider all sides of each argument, put the evidence on the scale, and make a stand for truth.

ABSTRACT

This publication addresses the frontiers of science and how the cutting edge of understanding reveals the reliability of God's word.

This book has been separated into ten chapters. Chapter one, Natural Doubts: the importance of addressing doubts. Chapter two, God's existence: why believe anything exists? Chapter three, Geological Column: the rocks cry out. Chapter four, Fossils: evidence frozen in time. Chapter five, The Grand Canyon: two catastrophic events make one beautiful landscape. Chapter six, Radiometric Dating: certainty or guesswork? Chapter seven, Cosmology: what does deep space reveal? Chapter eight, Epigenetics: what quantum biology is revealing. Chapter nine, The How and Why of Apologetics: Chapter ten, Six Literal Days: the impact of the book of Genesis Chapter One.

PREFACE

Since the dawn of mankind, we have searched the heavens for a god. Every civilization that archeologists have unearthed shows precipitous amounts of evidence of man seeking a higher authority. Despite the desires of atheists, agnostics, and evolutionists, humans continue their ardent pursuit of god(s). This concept befuddles the academics as they write books titled *Why God Won't Go Away: Brain Science the Biology and Science of Belief, Beyond God: Evolution and the Future of Religion*, the infamous Richard Dawkins's book, *The God Delusion*, and many more.[1] Regardless of one's belief in a god or declaration that one does not believe in a god, it is apparent every human must make the conscious decision to declare one certainty or the other.

Study after study reveals the same results: today's churches and Christian schools are not attaining their primary goal of making disciples. Instead, the already relatively small groups of students who enter these places of Christian education are eventually leaving their theological roots behind en masse.[2] A small percentage returns later in life, but the unfathomable number of defectors is not slowing and is likely increasing from year to year.[3]

It is important to note that while apologetics can have an effectual alteration to some students, to others, it is unlikely that any form or amount will change their view. For example, some high school students who are active in their church anticipate and often follow through, living a variant lifestyle once they enter college.[4] It is not that the students question their belief system and are missing a defense for their belief; it is their desire to *temporarily* live contrary to their moral convictions that propel their choices. Other students do not plan to ignore their religious beliefs, but the collegiate atmosphere and atheistic philosophical musings of professors alter their faith.[5] Professor Budziszewski states, "From the moment a student sets foot on the contemporary campus, their Christian convictions and disciplines are assaulted."[6] Reviewed as a whole, these studies reveal that attending college is not what alters one's religious beliefs; it is the chosen lifestyle, generally speaking, which has an overall negative impact on the ability of one to hold onto his or her childhood religious faith.[7] Regnerus and Uecker add to this defense when they write, "the college experience — more than the education itself — seems corrosive to religious faith only among those who were at an elevated risk of such corrosion when they arrived on campus."[8] Christian apologetics is more likely than not to assist those desiring to live a Christian lifestyle compared to those who willingly follow the wayward college and/or secular world regardless of college or career.

At a recent conference at a well-known seminary in Kentucky, an orator rightly asserted: "It seems as Christians, we are sorely behind in doing something about this trend [family-focused churches in lieu of person-centered], and the trend has already altered, but at least we are doing something now." Christians, similar to businesses, cannot afford to ignore a changing society and keep doing what they do because it's comfortable. While the Church sleeps, teenagers are determining their church and its beliefs are irrelevant and are walking away by the millions. Christians cannot ignore the fact that our youth are asking legitimate questions and receiving subpar responses from unprepared instructors.[9] Unless or until we get those two areas right, the Church will continue to see teenage church attendees leaving the church after graduation at alarming rates exceeding sixty percent.[10]

The aforementioned is a powerful incentive for the church to alter its academic course to include a focus on Christian apologetics. While there are many more reasons, the following are four compelling motivators: (1) God demands it; (2) reason requires it; (3) the world needs it; (4) we are His answer.[11]

First, God's demand is found throughout Scripture, but the battle cry of apologists is located in 1 Peter 3:15: "But in your hearts honor Christ the Lord as holy, always being prepared to make a defense to anyone who asks you for a reason for the hope that is in you; yet do it with gentleness and respect (NIV)." It is easy to miss the fact that this is a command, not a suggestion. Also, it is for all Christians to prepare and perform the defense of the gospel. It is not a requirement only for the so-called professionals; it is for all who name Christ as their Savior.

In addition to the need to recognize the demands of God in this verse, there are three additional aspects one should recognize for the *how* of apologetics: (1) the primary reason for apologetics is that it honors Christ as Lord. According to Scripture, our primary purpose in life is not to live for ourselves or even to obtain salvation; it is to honor Christ (Isaiah 43:7; 1 Corinthians 6:20; et al.). (2) We study and tell others why we believe what we believe because it convinces others of their need. This aspect fulfills, helps, and prepares the way for fulfilling the Great Commission set in motion by Christ Himself (Matthew 28:16). (3) We are to inform others about our hope with complete humility. That is, one's salvation from Hell is not possible without reaching a level of humility that directs one to comprehend and then admit one's inability to save his or her eternal soul from damnation from a righteous God.

This is not a call for us to defend God as if He is a weak and meager finite being who is defenseless. God is God, and His power and authority transcends all of creation. Many scholars attribute Charles Spurgeon, a popular British Baptist preacher of the mid-1800s, to making the statement, "Defending God is like defending a lion." One need only to open the cage and the King of the jungle will do just fine. While Spurgeon is a brilliant expositor of Scripture, I humbly call into question his intent with this statement. That is, if he was merely stating that God is beyond man's power to diminish or attack Him, I concur. If, however, his intent is to say that we do not need to defend our belief in God, I disagree. God, via the Bible, mandates a defense of His servant's hope or, said another way, why we believe God saves us from Hell (1 Peter 3:15). Why we believe we know the One true God exists (Jude 1:3). And why we are so adamant that the way of the Bible is the final authority over all other claims of truth (2 Timothy 3:16).

Secondly, reason requires apologetics. "But these people scoff at things they do not understand. Like unthinking animals, they do whatever their instincts tell them, and so they bring about their own destruction" (Jude 1:10, NLT). God does not desire unthinking creatures who stand for nothing and fall for anything. A reasoned response exists as to why I believe what I believe. Blind faith is the thing of cults, not Christians. The Creator God has left His unmistakable thumbprint on this planet and universe; one need only study to discover His handiwork.

The Christian faith is rational and logical in all aspects, and it is the only world religion that does not break the logical fallacy of the law of non-contradiction. Jonathan Edwards wrote, "While God wants to reach the heart with truth, He does not bypass the mind along the way."[12] We are to speak of truth because rational thought is the natural desire of man. We often fail to address the truth, which upholds our claims of fact despite the reality that supportive evidence abounds. Paul wrote, "Be transformed by the renewal of your mind, that by testing you may discern what the will of God is, what is good and acceptable and perfect" (Romans 12:2). We are to address the whole person, which includes the mind. Reasonable people rightly demand a reasoned response to the profound questions of life.

Our faith is not an irrational faith, but one based on the evidence leading to things that are not seen (Hebrews 11:1). Conversely, cults ask their constituents to follow them with little to no reasoning with the promise of exposing concealed information if they stay longer, try harder, or live better. God warns us of this when He says to "test the spirits" (1 John. 4:1). There are logical reasons why I am not a Scientologist,

Mormon, Jehovah's Witness, Muslim, et cetera. That is, I have spent years examining the wisdom, knowledge, and precepts of these ideals and found them wanting. I do not do well when someone asks me to blindly follow or informs me that I cannot understand because I do not have the right education or IQ. I do not have the acumen to know how a computer operates, but I certainly know when it does not work.

For example, Scientology is a financial pyramid scheme, requiring more money to obtain perfection or what they call *Clear*.[13] Mormonism contends secret rituals for the elite and sexual perversion (although publicly denied) of its male adherents in the form of polygamy.[14] Jehovah's Witnesses claim to be the only voice for God, yet their literature continually contradicts itself.[15] Islam teaches and uses brutal force, including murder, to spread the belief system (Quran, sura 2:190; 216; 8:36; et al.).

Thirdly, the world needs Christians who will deliver apologetics. One needs only to turn on the news, and she will quickly realize the depth of depravity of humankind. Without a Law Maker or Fence Maker, we cannot know where our boundaries are, minus the impromptu and ever-changing opinions of man.

Not only is mankind without a moral rudder without God, but we also have sensible questions that require an honest response. One of the greatest opportunities to spread our faith is when someone asks us a sincere question. There are those whose anger is so great that they are not attempting to obtain truth but, instead, to stir controversy and hatred. But for those who come into our midst in a church setting, it is a great opportunity to spread our faith. Christianity has its answers; the question then becomes: are we ready with an answer, or are we ill-prepared?

Lastly, we are His answer. "Bring them up in the training and instruction of the Lord." (Ephesians 6:4). This is one of the greatest mysteries of all time. The infinite God of the universe, who depends on nothing, needs nothing and relies on nothing, uses sinful, fallen, and finite mankind to spread His word. While inanimate objects could do His bidding (Luke 19:40), He has called on us to tell others so that some may be saved (Matthew 28:16-20). In particular, parents or those charged with overseeing children are under command to teach them about God on a continual basis (Proverbs 22:6; Deuteronomy 11:18-20; Ephesians 6:4; et al.).

As guardians of the next generation of Christians, we are the professors they rely on for their answers to tough questions. We can be like the deficient substitute who arrives to class late with a bad attitude and is untrained, or we can be the full-time professor who everyone wants. A teacher who engages the class psychologically is cognitively equipped, physically dynamic, and spiritually mature. Students are experts at spotting an inferior substitute and/or a hypocrite. One must come fully ready to participate in the education process known as apologetics.

It is important for the reader to understand that one of the greatest hurdles this writer had to overcome to accept Jesus as Savior was intellectual doubts. Society routinely confronts the world with scientific, philosophical, logical, and historical data that appears to contradict that which Christians claim as truth. It is directly due to said concerns that many avoid Christians or anyone who claims to understand absolute truth. This author does not take this subject as simply a professional adventure or a cerebral mountain to conquer for the sake of winning an argument. Apologetics helped save this writer's life, marriage, and sons' souls. This pursuit of knowing the ultimate truth is personal. It is because of this drive that this essayist writes the following about his testimony.

Within a few months of my conversion to Christianity, a relative sent me a few videos of Dr. Kent Hovind, also known as Dr. Dino. (Unfortunately, while some of his scientific work was brilliant, some of it is not, and I cannot recommend him as a resource.) Watching these videos excited my heart and mind, but, most importantly, they set me on an intellectual journey of intrigue to find out more. Before those moments, I had no idea that evidence substantiated the Bible. It was as if a switch flipped that started a burning desire to know more, and nothing was going to stop the momentum.

Over the last nineteen years, I have spent thousands of hours viewing DVDs of debates, studying various apologetic books, dissecting Scripture, and earning several degrees, including three advanced degrees from accredited universities, so I could know more about how science and God interact. I have had the privilege of teaching students from elementary through venerable adults in Christian schools, public and private universities, and various church settings. The degrees, time spent studying, and speaking in front of crowds only served to illuminate the fact that I have acquired a taste for depth, and it is insatiable. I am no longer satisfied with simply viewing the top of the ocean or standing on the shores; I want to dive deep and grasp its complexity, and the pull of its glory is seducing. The Psalmist wrote, "Deep calls to deep" (42:7). I am diving in.

It has become apparent that many people — similar to the way I was nineteen years ago — do not know that evidence for God, the Bible, and Jesus Christ abounds. They do not know that we, who are Christians, do not have to rely on circular reasoning, blind faith, or shallow statements that do not address one's intellect to follow Christ. The apostles, those who walked with God in the form of a man, Jesus, continuously asked questions, and Jesus always responded with love and warmth. Most importantly, Jesus gave an answer to their questions and to everyone who asked, except for Pilot. Pilot's inquiry, like many today, was not genuine, and his intent was self-serving. Asking questions is how education operates, and understanding God follows the same pedagogical pattern.

God, the Creator of humankind's cognitive abilities, knows we are curious creatures who rightly demand logical, inductive, and deductive thoughts to arrive at a given conclusion. It is due to said exigency that one does not believe certain existential claims or epistemologies. For example, I am not sitting under the tutelage of a Scientologist who espouses the theology of L. R. Hubbard because, upon studying their claims, I found them severely wanting. This line of cognitive dissection continues for all major world religions. It is the claims of the Christian religion alone that stand up to scientific, philosophical, theological, logical, rational, and historical analysis and do not falter at any point.

Some argue that Christians blindly follow their parents' musings or those of a given pulpit prognosticator. While this may be true for some, within Christianity, it is not necessary or recommended by the very Scripture they espouse to know; it is a personal relationship requiring a personal decision (Romans 10:9-10). I serve a Savior who provides His followers with data that satisfies my cerebral cravings so that I may know that I know.

CHAPTER 1
NATURAL DOUBTS

POLICE OFFICERS HAVE to put aside bias, concentrate on details, and consider all possible solutions to a given crime. A good detective follows the trail where the evidence leads and puts aside any preconceived notions.

The vast majority of crimes solved are not with incontrovertible evidence that leaves a jury with no doubts. Instead, prosecutors must show their case is true beyond a *reasonable* doubt. The implications of such a mandate are clear; it is okay to have some doubts about a given conviction of truth as long as they are reasonable.

Standing too close to a situation can lead someone to interpret evidence incorrectly. It is imperative that a person step back and view the scene in a holistic manner, slowly dissect the information, and only then should she begin to logically deduce a hypothesis as to what has occurred, moving her closer to a conclusion.

Doubts are natural and healthy; natural in the sense that when someone tells us something we have never witnessed, our initial response is to question that claim. Minus this cognitive protection, we are likely to follow any given philosophy. Doubting claims of truth is healthy because it can save us deep emotional regret, falling prey to various schemes, and unwittingly following a charlatan with malicious intentions.

A wise person will question claims of truth. The more daring the claim, the more one should slow down and further evaluate its foundation in truth. It is man's questioning that often keeps him from errors and misguided life choices; one must query to achieve accurate results.

Of primary concern is the fact that mankind cannot seem to satiate his desire to conjure up lofty ideas simply for the enjoyment of deceiving others. The root causes for lying are plentiful but often involve one's propensity to obtain power, wealth, and/or sexual pleasure. That is, when one studies some of the most grandiose declarations of truth through the centuries, these three influences are often prominent.

For example, in the Bible, Joseph's brothers sold him into slavery to remove him from his father, Jacob, so they could have the wealth of the family and the respect of the father. Emperor Nero blamed the Jews for burning Rome so he could retain power. And Catholics, at the origination of Roman Emperor Theodosius (379-395) and confirmed by Pope Gregory (600), claimed there is a place of suffering after death for those saved by God's grace called purgatory, which is not spoken of anywhere in Scripture. They claim one can shorten the length of time spent suffering in this location by paying indulgencies and novenas (money) to a priest. Joseph Smith's new religion of Mormonism allowed him to have sexual relations with many wives (the LDS church later declared polygamy wrong)[1]. The lies spoken behind closed doors by prominent politicians and blue-collar workers to acquire power, wealth, and sex through the centuries are innumerable.

Questioning truth is what leads one away from a path of destruction. When someone proffers reality, it is healthy and prudent to examine that claim to truth or risk being a fool or worse. Atheist astronomer Carl Sagan once quipped, "Extraordinary claims require extraordinary evidence."[2]

There are reasons why many are not Scientologists, Buddhists, Hindus, Christians, or follow Kabbalah — they have found their individual truth claims preposterous and not firmly rooted in reality. Christianity is one of the most illogical of all religious claims. That is, its core is a fearless yet audacious claim that a man rose from the dead for the remission of humankind's sins.

It is only after one is a Christian for an extended period of time that such an unscientific claim rolls off of one's lips as if he is talking about the color of the sky. One is unwise to out-of-hand accept that which is contrary to every known physical, logical, scientific, and historical piece of evidence known to mankind; that is, that a man rose from the dead.

There is a depth of wisdom when the Bible wants people to be cautious with claims of truth. It, in a real sense, asks humans to question everything. God does not call His people to be foolish, but instead wise as serpents (Matthew 10:16) and people who test the spirits to see if they are of God or the world (1 John 4:1).

Beyond the resurrection of Christ are multitudes of doubt producing stories in the sixty-six letters combined to make one book that we call the Holy Bible. Non-Christians, and some Christians, call into question the events of creation in the book of Genesis: a burning bush, the plagues of Egypt, a global flood, the miracles of Jesus, et cetera. The aforementioned and many more biblical stories should cause one to pause and consider their veracity. To doubt a grandiose claim is normal; to accept them without further inquiry is foolish.

THE IMPOSSIBLE IS POSSIBLE

Just because, however, a story sounds impossible does not make it so. Scientists, philosophers, and theologians generally agree there are only two choices to explain our existence. One, the universe exploded from nothing and came into existence via unknown causes roughly 14.3 billion years ago; or two, a creator was the unseen cause for our existence. A possible third option is that we came from aliens, but that option takes us back to points one and two as to how they came into existence. Creation being one of two possibilities, therefore, is a sensible study to find the truth.

Considering there are only two options, naturalism or creationism, not only is such a study therefore scientifically plausible, but what could be more exciting than digging into research and glimpsing evidence for God and/or God Himself? I hope we, as a human race, are not considering ourselves so wise and intelligent as to assume or believe that we have answered all the questions about our mysterious beginnings. Or worse, neglect one of the most critical questions of all time: From where/who did everything begin? Simply because we fear the possible answer(s) or that it appears beyond human understanding doesn't mean we should ignore it.

Why close the door to such a possibility just because it befuddles our intellect? Scientists and commoners discovered many mechanisms and scientific laws because they were willing to go against the roaring tide of popular thought and were willing to dream. Their imaginations, based on little more than a hunch, led to inventions that have altered the path of humankind.

If, and again, I say *if*, the second possibility of a Creator God is feasible, why would we not at least leave that door open just in case God wanted to walk through it? The percentage of individuals who understand how a MacBook Air works is minuscule at best. That fact does not preclude many researchers, computer geniuses, and business leaders from studying Steve Jobs' creations as well as Steve Jobs. We rightly study both.

One example is the flood story found in the Bible. For a multiplicity of scientific and logical reasons, such an event appears impossible at face value. Fossils, however, cover the earth by the millions. Fossilization only occurs under specific and rare circumstances, namely, lots of water and fast-moving mud. It is possible that a global flood could explain the existence of said dead things. Additionally, the Bible, as well as nearly every known culture to have ever existed, records a global flood where a small group of people survived.[3] An intense study of a global flood, therefore, has merit. After all, no serious geologist denies every inch of the earth's crust was covered by water at least once. The only question is: how was it covered? These stated few examples demonstrate that while one may doubt the validity of a claim to truth, doubts, however, do not remove the possibility.

POLICE DETECTIVES AND EVIDENCE

Regardless of where one cognitively stands in a given study, there are some processes that one must adhere to in order to avoid an inaccurate grasp of any scenario. Professional police detectives employ various techniques to dissect a crime scene for the purpose of understanding the truth. The goal of an investigator is unpretentious and straightforward; that is, he is to determine who, what, when, where, why, and how of a given situation. The process of finding truth in daily society — in every city in America and around the world — has stood the test of time in the most rigid of courtroom settings. These standardized tactics, therefore, can assist us in finding unadulterated truth as we study a variety of apologetic topics.

Both Christians and secularists have a common problem: all humans want to be correct, and this notion will often propel an individual to rush to judgment of a given scenario or question. One needs to be cognizant of this normal instinct and avoid it at all costs. That is, one cannot allow prejudice or preconceived assumptions to get in the way of finding the truth. Detectives must be deliberate when processing a crime scene, listen with discernment as to what a witness says or does not say, and scan the setting holistically, as well as dissect individual pieces of information and determine how they fit into the whole. These are a few cautionary steps amongst many that police detectives employ to make certain their case against a given suspect is correct.

Detectives apply the philosophical principle of Occam's razor. A very basic definition is the simplest answer is likely the correct answer (it is not fully accurate because there are many variations of "simple"). Sir Isaac Newton defines it as "We are to admit no more causes of natural things than such as are both true and sufficient to explain their appearances. Therefore, to the same natural effects, we must, so far as possible, assign the same causes."[4] In other words, the more complex one makes an answer, the likelihood of it being right reduces. For example, a ball rolls across the floor in front of you. You logically assume someone rolled it toward you. It is not likely the ball suddenly appeared suspended in space near your ceiling, fell to the floor, and rolled in front of you. The most basic answer is typically going to be the correct one, and if you begin to answer questions with complex scenarios, the answer often becomes bizarre.

Investigators learn to doubt what they hear and question what they see. They must suspect everything or risk arresting an innocent person. The answer is not always what it seems because things and people engineer and manufacture stories and evidence for a variety of reasons. Sadly, the scientific and theological communities are not immune from such nefarious motivations. From Hackle's fake drawings of embryos in an attempt to validate Darwin's claims to David Koresh's fake messiah claims to obtain power and sex, man has sought fame and fortune at the cost of integrity. Hence, for these reasons and many more, we are wise to rightly address our doubts in a judicious and methodical manner so that ultimate truth reigns. We must allow the evidence to dictate our direction, not preconceived wishful thinking based on our personal desires or the traditions of our parents.

NATURE OF EVIDENCE

The bottom line of all scientific inquiries, crime scene investigations, or theological debates is evidence. We use evidence every day of our lives. It is what helps us determine truth from fiction, right from wrong, and reality from illusion. I use a door handle to open a door because evidence informs me that door handles open doors. I use a key to start my vehicle because the evidence tells me keys start cars. Counselors determine the cause of a marital issue by the weight of evidence found within their clients' statements.

Evidence from various categories surrounds us daily. Our intellect and the power of the Holy Spirit are what assist us in living in the real world. If we ignore said reality, we remain in our own conjured-up world for our own temporal pleasure.

Atheists accuse religious people of living by blind faith. The Bible, however, speaks about God, who supplies His creation with evidence. In the book of Hebrews, chapter eleven, the writer states, "Now faith is the assurance of things hoped for, the conviction of things unseen." This verse is an image of what occurs in a courtroom.[5] That is, it is a legal setting where an attorney proffers evidence to the jury. It is reminiscent of Paul when he spoke to the Athenians (Acts 17). He used that which enveloped the people to demonstrate that there are things beyond those items that indicate their unknown God is the God of the Jews and/or the Bible.

People do not remain or become atheists from a lack of evidence; it is that humankind is too easily satisfied and stops short of possible answers to difficult questions. Of course, another possibility exists: we fear the conceivable answer behind door number two. It seems illogical and weak to stop one's search for truth just because the evidence trail becomes more spread out and difficult to follow and connect the dots. My desire is to follow the trail of crumbs until I find the truth, not just support a presupposition. Arriving at a conclusion is momentarily relaxing, but discovering the truth is eternally fulfilling.

Evidence is a large word with several gradations of meaning. A detective is not ready for the courts until she understands the levels of evidence. Evidence is what determines truth, not what one personally craves for personal worldview needs. While there are many forms of evidence, there are three primary types discussed in this chapter: (1) reasonable suspicion, (2) preponderance of evidence, and (3) beyond a reasonable doubt. All three are in use every day on our city streets and in courtrooms. Police officers and court officials employ these types of evidence for a variety of reasons, from the lowest of importance, e.g., making traffic stops, to the highest charge of any jury, e.g., capital crimes.

Reasonable suspicion is a low level of belief based on a small amount of evidence. It is "a pattern of abnormal or erratic behavior."[6] For example, a police officer can pull someone over when they observe a motor vehicle infraction. They detain people of interest when they obtain incriminating eyewitness testimony. Officers can delay a person when they observe behavior that leads them to believe something is wrong with the individual. In other words, reasonable suspicion is slightly higher than a hunch but lower than corroborating evidence. In scientific terms, a similar process is a hypothesis. The scientist observes a reaction, makes an educated guess as to why it occurred, and then begins to investigate further.

The second level of evidence is preponderance of evidence. This is when things are more likely true than not. That is, the evidence implicating an individual is greater than the evidence indicating that he is innocent.[7] The key is the overall weight or authority of the evidence, not the amount. For example, an intoxicated citizen's word versus a sober businessman's word. The courts will hold the clearheaded professional's recollection of events to a higher level than the man who could not stand due to inebriation. In science, this loosely relates to a theory. Scientists put a hypothesis to a test and the resulting evidence indicates that the hypothesis is accurate or not. If the results of the experiments substantiate the hypothesis, it becomes a theory. While a theory is a strong case for a scientist, it is not the strongest.

The final form of evidence in this project and Western society is the highest level a human can face in a courtroom beyond a reasonable doubt. The courts reserve this high level of certainty for criminal cases to include some of the harshest punishments humans can receive—a life sentence or death penalty. This definition, therefore, is critical to understand and is often misunderstood. That is, many believe this indicates that a person has one hundred percent certainty the crime occurred and the person on trial committed the same. This belief, however, is inaccurate. One hundred percent certitude is one hundred percent impossible on this side of Heaven. Beyond a reasonable doubt indicates there is room for some doubt, but it is reasonable disbelief to an ordinary person.[8] In scientific terms, this is akin to a scientific law. For example, water boils at roughly $212°F$. Scientists, however, have not tested all water at all locations around the globe or outer space. One of the strongest statements a scientist can make is that something is more likely true than not true.

POLICE AND SCIENTIFIC EVIDENCE APPLIED TO THEOLOGY

A person would be imprudent to believe the claims of a given religion are true if the evidence put forth was equal to reasonable suspicion but got no higher. Further, an individual is not thinking clearly if he follows a person and/or philosophy if they offer their facts and the influence of the evidence reaches a preponderance of evidence and no higher. There are simply too many unanswered questions at those levels that one must study for a decision to be cognitively valid.

The wise person will hold her philosophical and theological worldview standard of truth to the highest level known to mankind beyond a reasonable doubt. Anything less than this benchmark seems unwise and dangerous. Again, we are submitting to the agony of continued research and stopping short of the ultimate truth. Many factions of society vie for our attention and belief, from commercials to cults. We, as a species, are in danger of serious and perilous error when we do not rightly discern our surroundings with reliable corroboration.

The key to this measure of truth is that one can still have some unanswered questions and/or doubts as long as those questions are reasonable to an ordinary person. In the boiling water scenario, while a test of all water is not complete, it is reasonable to believe that water at some never-before-visited location will boil at the same temperature as the water coming from your tap.

While we do not have a video of Jesus walking out of the tomb (I submit that if we did, its validity would be called into question and doubted at the same level as it is today), it is reasonable to believe it did occur if we possess corroborating evidence. This book is not about the resurrection of Christ, but the evidence from the naysayers alone makes the resurrection of Jesus a plausible answer via a preponderance of the evidence. Further study moves the evidence beyond a reasonable doubt.

DOUBTS ARE HEALTHY

It is completely natural to have doubts. Anyone who does not have doubts would not likely live long, as he would continue to live a foolish life, taking unnecessary risks that would eventually take his life. The problem is not that one doubts; the glitch is when one does not address his doubts but, instead, allows them to linger. Where this can cause the most harm, eternally speaking, is theological.

One rightly questions someone who states that an invisible, all-powerful being exists, no one can see him, or he will die, and he had one of his kids come to earth for a while and then flew back to an unobservable location above us somewhere, and if we do not believe it, then we will go to an eternal place of torment. There should be all manner of doubts and questions in such wild claims of truth. If, however, one truly investigates the aforementioned and, despite the ridiculous nature, the assertion is found more likely true than not, then one's preconceptions must be set aside, and the facts must be followed to truly grasp reality.

For years, the medical field did not understand that blood holds the key to life and health. Bloodletting/phlebotomy was a common form of medical intervention, often leading to hypovolemic shock, myocardial infarction, and death of the patient (limited use of phlebotomy continues to be the best practice for specific disorders such as polycythemia vera). In time, the evidence against the strong force of this profession verified that bloodletting for gunshot wounds or colds and flu was not healthy and, in fact, was counterproductive to a physician's intent of healing. This is one example among many: the world is flat, the earth is the center of the universe, the creation of the Channeled Scablands in Washington was from slow glacier carving, et cetera.

Our collective scientific history abounds with examples where the politically strong advocates (religious and secular) won various scientific debates while the truth and/or evidence was set aside, oftentimes purposely. It was only after the evidence became so overwhelming and obvious to the masses that the attitudes of the powerful had to alter. Evidence should always dictate scientific laws and never majority rule and/or wishful thinking to retain political/financial authority. The key to this argument is that most proofs were available, but their worldview led them to preconceived assumptions instead of following the mandate of scientific empiricism. It is, therefore, our personal biases that must bend under the pressure of the facts and not our theories reading the facts.

CONCLUSION

Similar to the scientific advancements following the abundance of evidence, so it is with the apparent outlandish claims of

Christianity. That is, while the story of God, Jesus, and the Holy Spirit first appears preposterous, the evidence demands a verdict.[9] It is the contention of this book that the verdict can only be one way: God exists, Jesus rose from the dead, and the Holy Spirit is the third part of the Trinity that empowers man to live for God.

Everyone will have troubles, tribulations, and heartache. The fact that someone is a Christian is irrelevant to the struggles of this world, as God warns His creation to expect life to be difficult (John 16:33), and as such, bad things will happen to good people.

The issue is not why we face strife. The concern is why, after reading God's word and knowing full well what is coming do we, as Christians, not spiritually prepare for the coming crisis while the days are calm? The means by which mankind obtains proper training is via an overhaul of one's mind. The Bible calls this preparation a renewing of our mind (Romans 12:2). The Scriptures describe a person who gives one's life to God as someone whom God has given the ability to think and see the world with a new vision unaltered by a sin nature (Colossians 3:10).

It becomes the convert's responsibility to employ one's newly reborn skills to reprocess data through the lens of a Christian worldview. It is when one cognitively internalizes God's word that one's mind, for the first time, truly recognizes the reality of life. It is the first time in one's life when one can finally know what "pleases the Lord" (Ephesians 5:10). This has nothing to do with IQ or intelligence of any particular kind, but instead, knowing God helps one know oneself and the world in which one lives. But the data is not magically inserted into one's mind. Hence, the natural doubts will continue unless or until one spends time finding answers that satisfy the renewed mind of the believer. We will walk by the Dali painting and never see the dog, leaves, or tree.

Of primary importance in this battle for the mind is often that Christians do not spend the time addressing their doubts about God. Many will take the required step of faith for salvation and remain a spiritual infant. When life hits them with difficult situations that appear insurmountable and the physical and psychological pain is severe, their belief system often falters or fails. The issue is not that the facts changed; truth cannot change. The difficulty is the inability to accurately work through the issues because they have not properly prepared themselves for the tough times. Their doubts continue to exist due directly to unaddressed faith questions and/or doubts (Luke 8:4-21).

In the midst of a crisis is not the best time to address deep philosophical issues, nor is it the time to study the profound details of God. It is best to address our doubts in the good times when our logical and rational thought is most unencumbered. Then, when our feelings fail us, the knowledge we established in the past is what we cling to for assurance of things hoped for and the evidence of things unseen. To doubt is wise; to leave those doubts unaddressed is reckless and will often lead to a floundering, lifeless faith.

CHAPTER 2
GOD'S EXISTENCE

THE MOST DECISIVE and profound question one can ponder is: Does a creator god exist? The answer to this question, one that ultimately everyone must personally answer, changes everything. If a creator god exists, then this life has meaning, there is purpose, there is depth, there is love, and he/she/it has the right to question those created about what they did with the time they were allotted.

Archeological evidence demonstrates humankind's search for a god is an innate inquiry. That is, evidence of humans seeking and/or representing a god(s) is abundant in every society from the dawn of time. This search for the divine has often led to horrible ritual practices in an attempt to please their chosen divinity. Regardless of the outcome, humans cannot seem to escape the intellectual attraction of something greater than our mere mortal existence.

While this inquisition is indispensable, it is also likely the most difficult question someone can ask. We are like elementary students asking a medical doctor trained in brain surgery to explain brain surgery to us when we have just learned we have a brain. In other words, it is an exciting journey into intellectually deep waters where simple answers are not possible. The words and images we must use are going to be new and often confusing at first blush, but they are required to begin to perceive the unseen. We, therefore, must understand and embrace our human limitations and not use them as a means for denying something we cannot fully fathom. It is good for some to know how to perform brain surgery; it is essential for everyone to know God. It is not a quick process, but one that takes time, energy, and commitment to know the truth.

The Bible tells us that God has put within us the knowledge of Him (Romans 1:18-22); that is why we continue to search despite the attempt by some to discredit such ventures. If God is a figment of a creative mind's imagination, caused by a failure of synapses to address reality, then we are to be pitied, for we are merely advanced primordial soup that came from nothing and will return to nothing. There is no other choice. God either is or is not; there cannot be a third option.

It is logical and wise, therefore, to spend some of our existence and energy determining the validity of the audacious, if not insane, claim that an invisible God does indeed exist. This question is of such a magnitude I should not and cannot trust the opinion of others; it is an inquiry that I must search and come to a personal conclusion which must rest on nothing but reality and facts, as best one can comprehend.

For example, before rappelling off a soaring cliff, my guide telling me the rope is secure is not sufficient. I personally check the tie-ins, my harness, the figure-eight knot, and see the rope reaching the bottom because my life is valuable to me, but not necessarily to a guide. His grasp of *secure* may vary from my certainty. Why not verify anyone's stated truth?

While religious people wonder why atheists or agnostics cannot detect the God they perceive, the atheist/agnostic ponders why the religious see anything at all. Research indicates that the majority of religious people, believers, are most prominent in uneducated locales around the globe.[1] The study indicates that the rate of atheism drops in Sub-Saharan Africa, where mostly uneducated and religious beliefs prevail. Conversely, in highly educated regions such as Western cultures, atheism rates rise steeply to around forty and fifty percent.

Psychology Today refers to man's continual search for meaning in a god as an opium effect.[2] That is, humankind apparently finds comfort and solitude when they believe that there is something greater. In particular, this belief becomes stronger when a group is under greater stress, including natural or manmade problems. For example, following the events of 9-11, it was difficult, if not impossible, to find a seat in many churches across the U.S. This same response follows almost every large disaster, as it did after Hurricane Katrina and the tsunamis that devastated Indonesia and Japan.

Additionally, some anthropologists have found a correlation between an increase in religious practices and the need for increasing the size of a community. Religion almost always mandates marriage, and wedded couples typically want families. The goal of such a belief system is that society as a whole will benefit from abundant free labor as the children work in the fields and factories.[3] This study indicates that man is naturally promiscuous, leading to un-fathered and unruly, free-running children, and unsupervised children have negative side-effects on a community. The best way to get a man to settle down, stay with one woman, and thereby create a multitude of supervised (working) children, which benefits the community, is to create a religion that mandates such actions.[4]

Some psychologists believe that the idea of a god is simply

an invention of the mind to bring peace and comfort in times of need. Via evolutionary processes we have found it necessary to create an unseen force that is greater than we are who makes all the pains of this world bearable. If we believe there is something worth living for past the mundane of the day-to-day, then each individual will be more likely to assist the whole by working diligently toward the common good of all.[5]

New research in neurotheology (our brain and theological issues) studies the brain at the synaptic level in an attempt to understand why, as Dr. Newberg puts it, God will not go away.[6] Newberg boldly asserts in his book *Why God Won't Go Away* that man appears hardwired to believe that God exists. The more we seek a god, the more our brains believe in a tangible God of reality. We connect with fellow believers with our mirror neurons and limbic and autonomic systems. A believer, therefore, is not crazy as much as he is self-deceived into believing the ultimate reality is the existence of a real God.[7] The result is not that one is closer to her chosen god; instead, the culture is drawn closer together as they join each other in these plains of neuron-excited moments, seeking oneness and, thereby, joy and pleasure.

Conversely, theologians and some philosophers have argued for millennia that God is not a figment of our imagination, a conjured-up being to bring comfort or a synaptic misfiring. They state the existence and/or mandate of God's existence is logically sound, philosophically arguable, and historically accurate. A common apologetic is that we can empirically determine the movement of air via various tests. The wind, however, is in and of itself not observable. Only the corollary effect of wind is observable. Likewise, God is not viewable, yet His attributes and impact are readily detectable.

Bear with me for a moment as we wax philosophical. Aristotle argued that the being we call God is the first cause of all things. He breaks all causes into four primary categories. Those four causes are Material, Formal, Efficient, and Final. The Final Cause is the Supreme Cause or God. To prove that a Supreme Cause exists, Aristotle primarily relies on the teleological argument. This philosophical argument states that all dependent and/or unnecessary things (a chair, cat, human, planet, et cetera.) that exist have a cause, and consciously aware creatures seek to understand themselves outside of themselves.

That is, we hunt for meaning outside the confines of our physical being in some form of an ultimate being that transcends our being.[8] Unlike you and I, this transcendent being is not dependent, nor can it be; therefore, it is necessary or required for other dependent/unnecessary beings to exist.

THE COSMOLOGICAL ARGUMENT

Put on your cognitive seatbelts and prepare yourself for a thrilling philosophical ride. Recall how this chapter started: we are elementary students asking the brain surgeon to describe brain surgery when we just learned we have a brain.

The cosmological argument (CA) is philosophical in nature and sensibly demonstrates the logically mandatory existence of a greater being. It reasons that there is a first cause of all things, and the first cause must be uncaused, or that being would require an uncaused cause. One cannot infinitely regress (a never-ending look back in time) seeking a cause; eventually, there must be an uncaused cause that is not dependent but self-reliant in order to account for anything to exist. That is, one cannot continue to step back in time, viewing other unnecessary causes as the cause of said additional unnecessary causes. Because all unnecessary causes have a cause, at some point in history, a necessary and uncaused cause inescapably exists to begin all unnecessary causes.

Philosophers write this logical argument in two primary manners. The first has three steps; the second has four. The Kalam CA, also known as the Horizontal CA: (1) Everything that had a beginning had a cause. (2) The universe had a beginning. (3) Therefore, the universe had a cause.[9] The Vertical CA: (1) Contingent beings exist. (2) Their non-existence is possible, yet they exist; therefore, there must be a cause for their existence. (3) The cause of the contingent beings cannot rely on other contingent beings or a cause, for that cause would need to exist. (4) Therefore, there must be at least one noncontingent or necessary being in existence that caused all contingent beings to exist.[10]

Aristotle wrote one of the first examples of the CA when he penned that all things that move do so because something began to move them, including the four known elements (i.e., fire, water, earth, and wind). That something that moves the universe is what he calls *the fifth element* (yes, like the movie). This element is uncaused and eternal. It is the unmovable mover of all.[11]

Following Aristotle were many more philosophers through the centuries who agreed with the premise of the CA. Renowned Christian apologist Dr. Norman Geisler refers to the CA as "The beginning of the end for atheism."[12] It was not until Immanuel Kant in the eighteenth century that the CA came under serious attack and scrutiny as illogical. Kant's primary concern with the CA was his belief that it is dependent on the ontological argument, which he considers defective.[13] The ontological argument for the existence of God states: (1) God, by a matter of definition, is a perfect being. (2) The existence of a perfect being is either impossible or a logical reality. (3) The existence of a perfect being is not logically impossible. (4) If a perfect being is not a logical impossibility, then the existence of God is favored over his nonexistence.[14]

Kant argues against the CA, stating it is logically flawed. He states that the CA argument builds its case on faulty grounds; the conclusion, therefore, of the CA is inaccurate as well, according to Kant. Bruce Reichenbach, however, argues against Kant's accusations in that Reichenbach accuses Kant of incorrectly defining the "necessary being" of the CA as the same as what is found in the Ontological "perfect being." Kant continues the defense by stating the CA "necessary being" is one that, if it exists, cannot stop existing, and if it never exists, it cannot simply begin to exist. Conversely, the CA's "necessary being" is one of logical necessity, as one cannot infinitely regress using only "unnecessary/contingent" beings. [15]

It is this author's view that, despite Kant's customarily astute philosophical arguments, in this case, his argument is obtuse. For some reason, he moves dangerously close to the logical fallacy of an either-or argument when, in fact, there is a third option. That is, he draws a connection between two views that happen to address the same issue, a God, and then draws an illogical conclusion that because one argument is weak, the other one is as well. This is tantamount to saying the Dali Lama's or L. Ron Hubbard's definition of God is inaccurate; therefore, anyone who believes in God is also flawed. Despite Kant's efforts, the CA continues to create logical problems for the atheist/agnostic.

THE BIG BANG

Christians often decry the big bang (BB) theory as anti-biblical. Kurt Wise goes as far as stating that the BB is "atheistic."[16] Wise bases said comment on his understanding of the Bible's timeline of roughly six thousand years.

This writer respectfully disagrees with Wise and others who assert that the BB is atheistic. It is my contention that a

Bible believer should embrace the confirmation of a beginning; after all, is that not what the book of Genesis purports? The only difference between the two conclusions is the cause of the beginning of it all; either God or some unknown natural event triggered the BB. The logical inconsistency becomes apparent in that nature did not exist, yet a natural explanation for the start of everything is all a naturalist can assert.

The theologian, however, employs an unnatural yet necessary cause — God. The Bible boldly proclaims in a matter-of-fact manner that God is the Creator of all things. There is no defense of the existence of God found in the Bible; He simply exists. One could argue the apostle Paul defends the existence of God in the book of Romans, chapter one. He wrote that God is evident to all of mankind if one takes the time to consider nature (vv. 17-18). Further, one could state the Bible as a whole is a polemic for His existence. There is not, however, a book of the Bible where God's existence is defended via a philosophical and/or logical manner: It simply states, "In the beginning God" (Genesis 1).

It was not until April 23, 1992 — when the COBE space satellite confirmed that the universe was indeed expanding at unimaginable rates — that scientists uniformly agreed with the BB theory.[17] Many cosmologists fought the notion of expansion instead of contraction because of the logical argument that must follow. That is, if the universe is expanding today, at one point, it must have been smaller; thus, there had to be a beginning. A starting point supports what creationists have always said was true, "In the beginning God created the heavens and the earth" (Genesis 1:1). Astrophysicist George Smoot (Nobel Prize winner in physics, 2006), a fellow researcher for the COBE findings, famously told an interviewer about the universe expansion, "If you are religious, it's like looking at the face of God."[18] To be fair, Smoot was not making a religious claim; he was being intellectually honest that confirmation of a start appears to elevate the possibility of a beginning, as recorded in the book of Genesis, more likely true than not.

Naturalist scientists have feverishly been working on an alternative to the BB theory primarily because of its scientific problem of where time, space, and mass emanated. That is, every known scientific law confirms the law that nothing exists that does not have a cause. This scientific law is the Law of Cause and Effect. Because the BB is verified, it is evident the universe had a beginning; there must be something that caused the cause/beginning of all things.

A few examples of such considerations theoretic physicists are working on to explain the cause of the beginning are the Theory of Everything (TOE), String Theory, Expansion, multiverse, incredible bulk, bubble, et al. Scientists grasp the implications of not supplying the public with an alternative to a necessary being we call God; God was the unseen cause that brought all into existence and continues to sustain contingent beings.

This is not a God of the gaps theory; it is a logical conclusion to the evidence: we exist, we know we need a cause to exist, and we cannot infinitely regress with causes since we now know there was a start; therefore, there is no choice but to assert there is indeed an uncaused cause that caused it all. Even if one of the new theoretical theories is substantiated to some level, it brings us back to the question of what caused that cause. In the end, there is no alternative to the painful truth that an uncaused cause exists, and the title we give that power is God.

The arguments for the existence of a god create a philosophical and theological vacuum. This author contends, via the following six reasons, as detailed by Norman Geisler, that the necessary and noncontingent being we seek is the God of the Bible. (1) God is powerful. Mankind witnesses the immensity, intricacy, and perfection of our surroundings. Whatever authority caused our universe to come into existence must be powerful. (2) God is intelligent. It is not only the macro world that is beyond our comprehension, but it is also the micro world that baffles the greatest of intellects. The further we travel in space, and the more we magnify the quantum aspects of the cell, the more we realize the breathtaking complexity that is nature. (3) God is moral. Humankind continually seeks justice and fairness. Either humans have somehow evolved to believe stealing something that is not theirs is wrong (as one example of thousands), or the authority of the uncaused cause instilled moral value in His creation; this writer opts for the latter. (4) God is necessary.

The details of this chapter serve as a persuasive line of reasoning that a necessary, noncontingent, or uncaused cause must exist, and we call the same God. (5) God is unique. Similar to the impossibility of an infinite regress of contingent beings, the same argument is applied to God. That is, whatever caused the first cause cannot be contingent on another uncaused cause; there can only be one. The God of the Bible is one. (6) God is Lord over creation. Natural laws, elements, or processes cannot fully explain the universe. The being who created everything has exclusive rights. The uncaused cause rightly controls, directs, and determines the course of all He has caused. God is the supreme ruler and, therefore, Lord of all.[19]

CONCLUSION

I do not believe that a clear-thinking individual would think that a gun at a homicide scene simply appeared. There has to be a cause behind the effect. Someone was the cause, and I, as a detective, would want to know what caused someone to leave it there.

The empirical data supporting the law of cause and effect are all over this crime scene. The bad guy believed something about the other guy, causing him to get a gun and pull the trigger, causing the hammer to fall, a bullet to fly, and vital organs to be destroyed, with death being the final effect. The bad guy was caused to exist by his parents, his parents were caused by their parents, and on back we go. Eventually, there must be a first parent, but what caused the first parent? If we say natural causes, what caused natural causes? If we say, God, what caused him/her/it?

The answer is a logical one; there — out of logical necessity — must be an uncaused cause because all things that do not need to exist, yet exist, must be caused, and that initiating cause has no choice but to eventually be uncaused or the law of infinite regress (regress argument) is broken. We call that uncaused cause God. There is no way around the need for an uncaused cause if we are to make sense of anything because all things have a cause, including this seemingly convoluted yet logical paragraph. I am mentally tired from just writing it.

God's intentions for humankind are simple, yet man complicates them and thereby makes his own life more difficult. For example, God created the Garden of Eden in perfection, and man added one more fruit to his menu. God rules His people, and man wants his own human government despite the warnings of the Creator. God allows man to discover electricity, light, and various other life-assisting inventions, and man uses them to add unhealthy amounts of work hours to the week and will, at times, inappropriately exploit them to remain active at night, leading to various societal issues (Nothing good happens after midnight). Man discovers chemicals that help reduce pain, and we take this help and abuse the drug made to make life better, leading instead to a time of misery, pain, and difficulties. The list of taking that which God meant for good and turning it into unhealthy is lengthy.

God is the Master Creator of all things seen and unseen. This is not a blind leap of faith into the dark, but instead, one can base this decision on large amounts of evidence. Logically speaking, the cosmological argument satisfies the philosophical side of mankind. Historically speaking, all known civilizations record events of a beginning authority we call God as the cause. Scientifically speaking, all known scientific laws must be broken for everything to come from nothing, and each of the same laws holds true as we know them if God exists. Hence, it is scientifically acceptable to study and accept the only alternative to natural or unaided beginnings: God. And theologically speaking, it is what the Bible, Koran, and Pentateuch describe for humankind.

Believing, therefore, in a Creator we call God is not a form of dementia or illogical conclusion. Believing in God is part of our genetic makeup as God said it was in the book of Romans, chapter one, verse nineteen, and what science is now confirming, that our mind is wired to believe and take comfort in said knowledge. Such scientific confirmations support God's word; it does not refute it. This fact is yet one more example of humanity discovering something straightforward and twisting it to fit preconceived notions. That is, atheist scientists study humankind's brainwaves and discover our brains have an encoding to believe in God. While this appears uncomplicated, they confound the data and respond that it is merely chemical and physical as to why God will not go away instead of seeing a correlation between what God said thousands of years ago and the now-exposed validity of the same.

God warned us that mankind would disown and disavow the existence of God (Psalm 14:1). In particular, this notion will increase as the return of Jesus Christ gets closer (Matthew

24:12). We have medically accurate, scientifically verifiable, and cultural trends surrounding us that further substantiate the trustworthiness of the Bible. One's faith in the reality of God's existence should increase as science at every level exposes the certainty of God. Science is catching the Bible, not the other way around.

CHAPTER 3

THE GEOLOGIC COLUMN

IN THE CRITICALLY ACCLAIMED movie *Jurassic Park*, scientists were able to bring back several large extinct dinosaurs to populate a Pacific island. The title of this movie emanates from what scientists have labeled the geologic column (GC).

The GC is a layered horizontal map that geology, archeology, paleontology, and a variety of other disciplines depend on to make a multiplicity of relative dating decisions (relative dating is a general statement of sequential age compared to the more precise aging detection, called absolute dating, used in conjunction with radiometric dating methods). It provides a chart to follow as they unearth artifacts, bones, and rocks to determine evolutionary succession and age.[1] Large-scale events (e.g., mass extinction, geologic fraction, et cetera.) are the determining features scientists use to delineate one layer from the next. These scientists attempt to understand what occurred in the past so we can better anticipate the future and not make similar mistakes.

To geologists, Earth is an oversized laboratory in which they conduct their experiments and literally collect tons of evidence. Geologists recurrently sift, examine, and occasionally send geologic material to a lab for closer inspection. Regardless of one's worldview (e.g., secularist or religious), the evidence gathered does not alter to fit the preconceived notions of the gatherer. That is, all geologists and all of humankind have the same information; it is only the interpretation of said evidence that differs.

It is no different from when a crime occurs, and two detectives view the same evidence but arrive at two different conclusions. It is not that one is attempting to mislead the other or vice versa, nor is one hiding evidence from the other; one answer is simply a different possibility from the other. No one holds secret proofs or clandestine labs where only atheistic and/or agnostic scientists work, giving them a corner market on truth. The argument that there are scientists and then there are the conservative religious folks has grown old; scientists are scientists, and, similar to other fields, variant conclusions are drawn from the same tests.

Scientists, both believers in God (which is roughly 40% of all scientists[2]) and those who do not see God in nature, study, dissect, and catalog the same evidence from the same geologists, archeologists, anthropologists, and biologists. The only variation is the interpretation of said evidence. There are always two sides to a story, in particular, when that story happened: thousands or millions of years in the past.

HISTORY OF THE GEOLOGIC COLUMN

One of the most critical elements geologists employ in their attempt to decipher the world around us is the geologic column (GC). The GC is a type of horizontal map or upright chart of sedimentary history (layers of dirt). It consists of all ten Phanerozoic layers, each one representing tens of millions of years of sedimentary deposition.

The complete GC is found in very few locations around

the globe (less than one percent of the earth's surface).[3] One interesting aspect, however, is the thickness of each layer is significantly less than theorized and required. That is, the entire GC, according to OE geologists, should be between 100 and 200 miles thick, and the average thickness at said 1% locations around the world is roughly one mile.[4] That means that only .5%-1% of what evolutionists theorize they should/must find is actually found. Statistically speaking, this is a negative Z-score outlier with no correlation. In common language, the GC thickness theory is fatally flawed and left wanting.

Given the complete lack of empirical evidence, the best place to view the hypothesized GC is in a textbook, as it is the only place on earth where it is known to exist. Its original creation emanated in the late 1700s and early 1800s by James Hutton and Charles Lyell (others contributed, but these two men are often given credit for the GC. All of us stand on the shoulders of giants and simply put together that which others have uncovered, but never created).[5] A key concept called uniformitarianism, or the geologic processes we observe today are the same as they were in the past, is the GC's basis for existence. In fact, it is referred to as "one of the fundamental principles of earth science."[6]

While anyone with a high school diploma understands the basics of the GC, very few grasp the near complete dependence the GC scientists have on their predictions and what they are finding in the field. That is, when submitting a fossil for radiometric dating, one of the questions is, "General Geographic Location: (Required for calibration of carbonate samples — not required for calibration of organic samples)" and "Stratigraphic and environmental details: (Please attach drawings and additional text)."[7]

It seems odd that a radiometric dating lab requires an answer to a calibration question and desires an understanding of the rocks or fossils that surround the sample for testing. One would think that after decades of scientifically calculating dates of fossils and sedimentary rocks, the mass spectrometer would not need to know the original location of the sample and the surrounding objects. At a minimum, these lines of inquiry call into question the validity of uniformitarianism (see below). In fact, the lab's website publishes several *assumptions* of radio-carbon dating that can play havoc with dating accuracy.[8] For example, a police officer does not ask the speeder how fast they think they were going so that they know; no, he already knows the answer based on empirical evidence. The driver's answer to that question is irrelevant to the known data.

A commonly held scientific belief prior to the 1800s was that the earth's crust moves rapidly — catastrophic plate tecton-ics.[9] Prior to the word catastrophism, scientists called the belief Neptunism.[10] The word itself derives from Greek and Roman mythology. That is, Neptune is the Roman god of the sea (or the Greek god Poseidon).[11] The proponents of this theory tell us that during the rapid plate movements, rocks formed by the crystallization of minerals in the oceans, and these forces created the land features we observe today. Many academics credit such beliefs, as endorsed for centuries, to the ruling class of Christians who believe in a Noahic Flood as found in the Bible.[12] The Greeks — similar to other cultures — believed that one major catastrophic flood event was responsible for much of the current geology.[13]

Other scientists observed the same large-scale extinctions and, likewise, believed catastrophes killed them, but not as the Bible or Greek mythology purports. One such scientist is anatomist and paleontologist Georges Curvier. His studies of mass extinctions and fauna succession led him to believe that time is dotted with catastrophic events, which led to what one observes in the geologic layers.[14]

Most historians credit Curvier with creating what would be the building blocks of the GC, an idea he called stratigraphy.[15] In Curvier's opinion, the crust of the earth divides and sub-divides into layers of time. Each of these layers, or strata, contains specific flora, fauna, and rocks. As scientists travel the world and dig into the crust, they locate identifiable regions similar to other areas of the world and thereby have the ability to determine what strata layer they are digging. Stratigraphy offers geologists a way of detailing strata gradations from one time to the next.[16] The world thus contains layers of strata containing fauna that are comparable to fauna in other parts of the world. Scientists can, therefore, compare a variety of exposed strata layers to determine similarities hundreds of miles apart.

The father of modern geology, James Hutton, was a farmer and canal builder turned geologist.[17] As he would plow the fields and observe various land features in and around streams and rivers, he took note of the strata. After leaving his farms to build canals, he continued to study the earth's crust, trying to grasp what the strata indicate. It was his conclusion that, unlike the belief of catastrophism, plate movement is an extremely slow, if not imperceptible, geologic process. Said movements brought about today's landscape, not abrupt alterations.[18]

Hutton's published beliefs stirred a paradigm shift and thereby the focus of geologists. They began to seek answers via slow geological processes and abandoned catastrophic movements. Similar to the slow process Hutton was proposing, his belief did not alter all of geology overnight, but the process had its official start.

One of Hutton's most famous quotes responsible for influencing geology as a whole was, "From what has actually been, we have data for concluding with regard to that which is to happen thereafter."[19] Later, another architect of modern geology, Charles Lyell, would coin a simplified version of Hutton's phrase when he penned, "The present is the key to the past."[20] With this bold statement, Hutton challenged the scientific community with its current belief system of catastrophism. That is, we see minute alterations requiring extended periods of time as opposed to large-scale and sudden changes. His belief is that no geologic evidence specifies that the movements we see today were any different yesterday or anytime in the distant past.

Half a century later, Charles Lyell read Hutton's works and agreed with his conclusions. He, like Hutton, was convinced that the present is the key to the past and there exists no empirical evidence to lead one to conclude the catastrophes of the past are the cause of the structures and traits found in geologic features. One needs only to measure the current speed at which geological features currently create and migrate to know what tomorrow will bring. Conversely, using the same evidence, one can extrapolate backward and make determinations as to what occurred in the past.[21] Geology, Lyell declared, should use available empirical data, not presupposition beliefs based on biblical or Greek mythological accounts, to make calculations of what will be tomorrow. To employ the apparent guesswork based on religious presuppositions is foolish.[22]

Another significant figure who began to change geologic perceptions is George-Luis Leclerc, commonly known for his French last name, Buffon. His observations in geology concluded that the earth is much older than the beliefs held by Neptunists. Leclerc put forth the notion the earth is at least 75,000 years old and not 6,000.[23] His work was a strong influence on fellow geologists who believe the earth is not only older than once thought, but one can read the succession of the process in the layers of strata.

It was the theories set forth by scientists such as Curvier,

Hutton, and, in particular, Lyell that brought about permanent changes in mainstream science. That is, science began to shift from catastrophism to slow processes. As one investigates this case, it is important to note the succession of events. One person puts forth an opinion, another builds on the same, followed by others who quote from and rely upon the previous thoughts. A structure's strength is in its foundation. If the base is weak, the structure will be weak. As one considers the footing of these individuals, given the technology and background available to them, is it reasonable to reconsider their certainty?

It was the work of these pioneers that led another scientist, William Whewell, to coin the term uniformitarianism to describe the dawdling processes. Whewell did this as he was reviewing Lyell's work and made a determination that Lyell's focus was really a uniform process of change that does not alter over time.[24] Similarly, but at the opposite end of the geologic spectrum, it was Whewell's review of scientific journals supporting Neptunism that led him to coin the phrase catastrophism.[25]

From these watershed moments and a plethora of other pioneering scientists, the foundation of the modern idea of the GC emerged. It is this new worldview that completely alters the strongly held, and some would argue scientifically backed, beliefs of the past few millennia, i.e., catastrophism. The GC has become the bible of modern geology. It is a primary tool created by a few men, using flawed, outdated techniques, wild conjecture, and grandiose juxtapositions to arrive at a poor conclusion.[26]

GEOLOGIC COLUMN DIFFICULTIES

Science is science, data is data, and the only variance between two opposing views is the interpretation of the evidence. Generally speaking, no scientist (i.e., Old or Young Earth) has more data than the next. For those who spend their lives studying this material yet arriving at different theories as to how and why "X" occurs, this is largely due to their worldview, not typically a lack of data and/or intelligence.

The following is a discussion of seven Old-Earth difficulties that assisted in the creation of the GC. I will demonstrate to the reader a variant reading of the same evidence and allow the reader to determine the validity or lack thereof of Old-Earth theology/geology. While this list is restrictive, it is sufficient to demonstrate to the reader that this debate is not settled, and further personal research is advisable.

One: Observational science (as compared to historical science, again, cosmology, geology, paleontology, paleoanthropology, and archeology) is discovering that rocks can form rapidly. Part of the uniformitarian theory is that rocks and fossils require long periods of time to form; millions of years are the accepted timescale.[27] This term, in general, recognizes the present is the key to understanding the past. For example, as scientists study the current speed of tectonic plate movement, sediment deposition rates, stalactite and stalagmite growth rates, et cetera, they can then know how old some objects are or how long a given tectonic plate took to get from position A to present position B. It is determined if things move, grow, and change at the known rates of today, then we can know how long it took to get to our present state of being.

The primary problem with this theory is that we cannot

know for certain, or with much precision, that such a belief is accurate. In fact, a well-known axiom, *One thing is for certain, the only constant is change,* is familiar because everyone finds it to be true. In fact, many scientists and some of the public decry that the world's climate is altering so rapidly that, if we do not do something to curb it, we are in danger of unimaginable human and animal catastrophe.[28] While the cause of such change is up for grabs, the reality of its adjustment, long or short-term, is clear. Environmental change is one example of continuous alteration that surrounds all of creation.

Additionally, scientists are discovering the earth can move at much faster rates than once thought. The key is not time but, instead, the surrounding available minerals, water, and various other required items in the correct ratio, and rocks and fossils can form rapidly.[29] For example, a set of car keys from a vehicle made in the 1960s is completely encased in solid rock.[30] A sailing ship, the *Isabella Watson,* sank off the coast of Australia in 1852.[31] Her metal bells were recently located near the wreckage in one meter of water. In only 150 years, sand and sea creatures hardened around the bell several inches thick, forming solid rock.[32]

These items are just two of many examples of artifacts found in rock that are not even close to thousands of years old, let alone millions. The encased items expose the reality that maybe all is not what it appears. When a scientist makes a definitive statement that something takes millions of years to form, it is not anti-intellectual to question said statement. At a minimum, these items reveal the veracity that rocks can and do form rapidly and do not require millions or even thousands of years. Perhaps Hutton and the judgments of others about uniformitarianism are not an open-and-shut case; perhaps the sages had it right with catastrophism. Perhaps.

. . .

Two: Scientists locate fossils in strata layers where they should not be found, GC speaking. Unfortunately, due to worldview paradigms held by the ruling class of Western scientists (e.g., Old-Earth evolutionists), articles controverting their view, once published in peer-reviewed scientific journals, are no longer permitted. Many other cultures do not permit this biased standard and publish antithetical theories as they seek the truth.

An example of the aforementioned is a book by two archeologists from India. Scientists Cremo and Thompson searched the world, looking for evidence of mankind. What they uncovered was a menagerie of human artifacts out of GC sequence as anticipated by *the establishment*. A few examples: (1) a metallic grooved sphere resembling the earth carved from stone with intricate detail found in pre-Cambrian soil, soil purported to be at least 2.8 billion years old. (2) A coin in Illinois buried in soil one hundred fourteen feet deep. The Illinois State Geologic Survey dates the surrounding soil at 200,000-400,000 years old. Someone did not purposely bury the coin, as the surrounding dirt is undisturbed. (3) A piece of metal embedded in marble with raised letters near Philadelphia, PA. Scientists have dated the mined marble at no less than 500-600 million years old.[33] Their book continues with similar evidence for nine hundred pages, with profound implications on Old- and Young-Earth theories.

Three: There are rock layers that are bent (as opposed to broken) to varying degrees, which is not geologically likely if the deposits hardened prior to receiving enough pressure to bend them. Geologists observe bent strata in the GC in nearly all locations around the globe. Uniformitarians attribute these odd features to heat and pressure placed on the layers after hardening occurred.[34] They hold to such interpretations due in part to uniformitarianism and thus long-age beliefs. Such stories sound fine until one applies the necessary mechanics and inconceivable odd events in dozens of locations around the world that would have been necessary to make this occurrence even likely, let alone plausible.

What geologists find are strata in numerous locations around the globe, with exceedingly curved or bent layers at incredible angles. The laws of physics state that these strata layers were not hard at the time of the bending forces, but instead, while the layer was still moist, soft pressure curved the wet strata.[35] Otherwise, logic and mechanical engineering mandate such incredible bends would break, crush, or show slips in the rock layers. A key is that rocks exposed to large amounts of heat and pressure (i.e., the kind required to make bends without breaking, crushing, or slipping) have evidence of such mineral alterations. Said evidence does not exist in the bent strata in most locations; instead, the rock layers appear to have been moist and cool at the time of the bend.[36]

One example (there are too many to list all of them) of strata bending on a large scale is in the mountains surrounding the Sullivan River in southern British Columbia, Canada. Mechanical Engineer and National Science Foundation Fellow Dr. Walter Brown exposed the engineering incapability of natural forces to bend the Sullivan River Mountains at the roughly 140-degree angle without the rocks breaking. Uniformitarian scientists attempt to describe how such bends and uplifts occur but said explanations do not match what geology and physics empirically know. That is because known scientific laws do not substantiate such claims; one must jump to large-scale conjecture to believe such conclusions.[37]

. . .

Four: Paleontologists have been digging into the earth's crust for more than one hundred and fifty years in search of evidence that would further support the Darwinian theory. One of the items they seek is the elusive transitional fossil, which is one creature buried and preserved in the process of turning from one organism to the next. While there is a small group of fossils that are questionable, we do not find the anticipated levels of thousands, if not millions upon millions, of transitional fossils. One frustrated scientist, Charles Darwin, wrote, "... the distinctions of specific forms and their not being blended together by *innumerable* transitional links, is a very obvious difficulty" (emphasis mine).[38] A fellow evolutionist of Darwin, Dr. Woodruff, decades later also lamented, "But fossil species remain unchanged throughout most of their history, and the record fails to contain a single example of a significant transition."[39]

Despite untold thousands upon thousands of man-hours across multiple continents, what continues to baffle scientists is the near complete lack of the required (according to Darwinian and neo-Darwinian theory) transitional fossils; they are not there as is predicted and required to support their theories. Perhaps the answer is simple: the theory does not work, and science must rethink other possibilities or create something new that fits the evidence. Eldra Solomon wrote this about Evolutionists:

"Because of the nature of the scientific process, each fossil discovery represents a separate "test" of the theory of evolution. If any of these tests fail, the theory would have to be modified to fit the existing evidence."[40]

. . .

Five: Scientists have continually unearthed the sudden appearance of fully formed and fully functional creatures by the millions. Scientists commonly refer to this event as the Cambrian Explosion (CE).[41] The reason for the title, as given by scientists, is because the fossil record documents that life exploded into existence, as opposed to what evolutionists not only predict but also demand in order to substantiate said theory. The CE does not even reach the level of wild conjecture, let alone evidence, for long periods of time or slow processional evolution. It is, instead, powerful evidence for the biblical account of creation in that there was a time when no life was in existence, and suddenly life exploded onto the scene from nowhere. From absolutely nothing, life began. Sound familiar? Read the book of Genesis, chapter one, which is one of sixty-six books or letters bound together into what we call the Bible.

Charles Darwin bemoaned the seemingly impenetrability of the CE conundrum. Darwin wrote,

"The abrupt manner in which whole groups of species suddenly appear in certain formations has been urged by several paleontologists — for instance, by Agassiz, Pictet, and Sedgwick — as a fatal objection to the belief in the transmutation of species. If numerous species, belonging to the same genera or families, have really started into life at once, the fact would be fatal to the theory of evolution through natural selection."[42]

Scientists continue to write about and discuss in Modern Neo-Darwinian literature the same concerns Darwin held. They continue to work on various theories to overwrite the obtrusive enigma the CE provides. However, the more they dig, research, and apply known and/or inferred geological principles, the more they further substantiate the validity of the CE. The infamous ardent and militant atheist Richard Dawkins wrote,

"And we find many of them [Cambrian fossils] already in an advanced state of evolution, the very first time they appear. It is as though they were just planted there, without any evolutionary history. Needless to say, this appearance of sudden planting has delighted creationists."[43]

[Please note the bias: creationists. They are actually Ph.D. scientists who study the same evidence and simply draw a different conclusion; something or someone started it all from nothing, and the evidence seems to support the same.]

Six: Fresh tissue and intact bone marrow cannot and should not be found in dinosaur bones if the premise that dinosaur extinction occurred roughly sixty-five million years ago is correct. That is, observable and repeatable science easily solidifies this belief. Blood in a dead creature rapidly deteriorates, dries, and is no longer pliable. This is such a well-known and unheated statement that no one who believes something that has been dead for more than a few thousand years (if not less) would even consider looking inside a given bone for soft fleshy tissue; it simply cannot exist.

On March 24, 2005, astonished paleontologists found fresh tissue and bone marrow when they accidentally dropped and broke open a *T-Rex thighbone*.[44] They sent the soft tissue to two labs to confirm the finding: one in North Carolina and the other in Colorado. Both confirmed the materials were elastic veins and pliable bone marrow. [45]

Mary Schweitzer, a lab scientist in North Carolina,

remarked, "Ostriches that died six months ago are producing structures that are similar to dinosaurs that died 70 million years ago,"[46] Schweitzer was freely speaking her mind based on her extensive working knowledge of studying bone.

This author submits that something is wrong with the paradigm, not the evidence. Everything we know in operational science tells us such a finding is not possible if the bones are millions of years old, but apparently, it is plausible. Bones, therefore, found at deeper levels in the GC do not necessarily indicate great age but may, in fact, call into question the building blocks of the GC (keep in mind how the GC was created, as discussed in the last section).

Seven: Scientists have found polystrate fossils, or upright trees, in various locations around the world that span multiple strata layers. One indispensable principle of the GC is the painfully slow succession of strata layers gradually overlaying one layer to form another. Uniformitarianism demands a leisurely process for such things to occur, as opposed to catastrophism, which supports the rapid layering of strata. Polystrate fossils go contrary to known physical and biological laws and counteract this key principle of uniformitarianism. Slowly covered dead trees do not remain upright for millions of years. Operational science — even a child — recognizes that trees die, fall down, decay, and then various organisms devour them. Further, specific and rare catastrophic circumstances must exist to cover fallen trees rapidly enough to fossilize them prior to the natural decay process. The enormous hurdle for uniformitarian scientists is that there is only one known method for polystrate fossilization — sudden and abrupt catastrophe. The notion that trees will remain intact as dozens, let alone millions of years pass, slowly covering them with dirt, is untenable to the logical mind. It takes great leaps of justification to consider anything variant.

GC supporters claim that these trees had their roots covered in peat, and then the trees died, leaving only the stump, which was then covered in mud, preserving the tree upright. While there are multiple problems with this theory (e.g., trees sit on top of coal seams with no root system entering the coal, well-preserved leaves surround the trees, et cetera.[47]), the most logical hurdle is that these trees are sometimes over ten-foot-tall and penetrate multiple strata layers representing millions of years. No known scientific law would allow an exposed piece of lumber to remain for millions of years while slow-moving dirt gradually covered the entire height of the trunk. At a minimum, the tree would take on a different shape or show signs of various stages of degradation. Instead, these polystrate fossils are nearly the same from bottom to top, as if the tree was quickly covered and frozen in time, and its penetration into multiple strata layers further indicates the environment laid down the variant strata layers in short order so fast that the leaves did not have time to rot. I would respectfully ask readers to consider their working knowledge of trees that die. Is it logical that the leaves would remain on a dead tree for days, years, decades, and longer? Would the tree remain standing while dirt covers its base — and eventually the entire tree? You decide what sounds logical based on empirical data and logic based on known facts, not conjecture.

Possible Explanation for Polystrate Fossils via Observed Data

Mt. Saint Helen gave scientists a glimpse of what Mother Nature can do during a cataclysmic event when it erupted in May of 1980. Following said eruption, large-scale deforestation took place, and a sizeable lake, Spirit Lake, became a much smaller lake as mudflow and several metric tons of trees inundated its banks. At first, the trees floated flat on top of the water. As the trees became waterlogged, the heaviest part of the tree, the trunk, sunk below the surface, causing the trees to float upright. In time, the trees descended to the bottom of the lake, some with enough force to cause them to enter the newly laid soft lake bottom. Mud continued to flow into the lake over the next few months at various speeds and times. When scientists explored Spirit Lake with scuba gear, they found trees buried in what appeared to be various strata layers, giving the appearance of age.[48] Given time and additional mudflows, one can theorize these trees will look nearly identical to the polystrate fossils geologists observe around the world today.

At a minimum, such evidence should call into question the strongly held belief of uniformitarianism leading to the building of the GC. Perhaps what geologists can empirically dissect and what observational scientists directly perceive should hold greater weight than what historical scientists suggest via estimation based on a paradigm or presupposition.

CONCLUSION

The GC is an intriguing concept and one fraught with difficulties. This chapter exposes some of the concerns scientists have for a theory with the number of variables, assumptions, and, at times, guesswork (e.g., relative dating methods for sedimentary strata use igneous rock below, above, or, sometimes, large distances from the product in question).[49]

Uniformitarianism does not appear, despite over a century of scientific exploration to do so to answer geologic anomalies. Conversely, catastrophism, while at times difficult to grasp the magnitude of the source and power of such cataclysmic events, seems to answer the difficult questions with greater scientific precision. Nearly covering the earth with frozen water is not a problem for uniformitarians (ice ages); they do not, however, like the idea of liquid water doing the same thing (i.e., a global flood). This book contends that this hesitation is not scientific in nature but, instead, a presupposition worldview that responds adversely to any theory that sounds vaguely comparable to a biblical account.

There is a plethora of supporting data for both theories and intelligent scientists continue to debate the minutia of both theories. It seems wise, therefore, for the observer to take a step back to the hypothesis stage instead of the theory level. That is, it is prudent and part of the scientific process for one to contemplate what each of the theories, uniformitarianism or catastrophism, should expect to find prior to putting one shovel in the dirt.

If catastrophism is accurate, one should expect, at a minimum, to find the following seven geologic features around the world: (1) The world, at nearly every altitude and extreme depth, must contain millions of dead creatures. A worldwide flood would necessarily consume all living life, including some sea creatures (the slow or immovable being the most prevalent), and entomb a small percentage of same to become fossils. (2) A few locations around the world should contain massive burial grounds. For instance, large sections of forests churned together with other vegetation and an occasional massive grouping of a large variety of animals buried alive and entangled in death. (3) Strata or sedimentary layers that run for more than a few hundred yards or miles but instead extend from state to state or country to country. A large-scale flood carries debris as far as the floodwaters travel. It is logical, therefore, to anticipate strata lines over a high percentage of a given continent. (4) In addition to strata layers extending for hundreds of miles, one should anticipate locating vegetation, rocks, or other flora, fauna, and animals normally located in one region of the world carried hundreds if not thousands of miles from their known climate and region. (5) Because of the extremely slow process of uniformitarianism, one would expect to find large-scale events recorded in the strata lines. In opposition, catastrophism swiftly inundates an area with new material so rapidly that strata lines do not have time to record local flooding events (localized water erosion marks), wind erosion, and various other evidence of long exposed sediments. Strata must, therefore, show little to no evidence of local erosion events, as such moments could not occur during a global flood. (6) Strata lines will bend and not break in small hills and large mountains. This abnormal feature occurs during a large flood when sediments fill with water, making them pliable, moveable, and susceptible to molding and shaping by exterior forces (as evidenced following the Mt. St. Helen eruption). Compare this expected outcome of catastrophism to uniformitarianism, where soil slowly moves into its current location, remains there for millions of years, completely solidifies, and at some point, the earth applies force to the strata. In scenario one, one expects bending, and in scenario two, one expects breaking of the hardened rock. (7) High-altitude photography will reveal geologic features concurrent with high water volume runoff. If a flood covers landmasses, it must return to the lowest point possible. Evidence of naturally occurring ponds and/or lakes running off and moving toward the oceans, which are now empty, should occur in various locations around the globe. Additionally, the oceans should have indications of being significantly shallower, as the waters from higher land areas would take hundreds of years (at a minimum) to reach a form of equilibrium. It is possible that humankind would build cities or roadways in the once-dry land. As the oceans began to return to normal depths during high mountain lake runoff, the waters would subsequently submerge said cities and/or roadways. It is possible, therefore, for anthropologists and archeologists to read about and possibly locate cities slowly consumed by the rising ocean waters. Humans are smart enough to move from the area, and the water would not drown or fossilize them, as the process would be slow. As the runoff continues, areas that were once inhabitable by humans due to plentiful water sources will dry up. We should, therefore, locate evidence of civilizations in now-arid locations yet containing geologic evidence indicating water was once plentiful.

Each one of the seven aforementioned expected results of catastrophism directly or indirectly opposes what uniformitarianism anticipates. This book submits that all seven anticipated catastrophic results exist in multiple areas around the globe. This author, therefore, believes the preponderance of the evidence weighs heavier for catastrophism than uniformitarianism. As discussed in this book, the GC relies profoundly on the reality of uniformitarianism for its subsistence.

Given the validity of this statement, one should, at a minimum, call into question the trustworthiness of the GC and consider the alternative, as there are only two choices: catastrophism or uniformitarianism.

CHAPTER 4
FOSSILS

FEW ITEMS MESMERIZE our imagination more than massive dinosaur fossils towering over us as we enter a museum. Our minds race with thoughts of a T-Rex hunting us. Slight fear grips our reflections of clever creatures like the velociraptor, working in packs to stalk our every move as they methodically set us up for the kill. Invading our thoughts is the invariable sign that typically reads, "Dinosaurs went extinct at least sixty-five million years ago ..." With such a large claim to knowledge, it is wise for one to ask how paleontologists know when dinosaurs ruled the earth.

Dinosaur fossils excite our imagination and are truly amazing. Similar to a bone-littered crime scene today, they offer a great deal of information from which we can construct a hypothesis that the public/jury can then test. They are well-preserved pieces of evidence of history for scientists and others to marvel at and study.

In nearly every corner of the world, it is possible to locate fossils. Scientists and residents planting trees in their backyards find these hardened skeletons at the highest peaks and the lowest valleys, from the ocean floor to the dry desert. In some geographical locations, one cannot stick a shovel in the ground without striking a fossil.

FOSSIL FORMATION

When considering the abundance of fossils, it is vital to realize that it takes abnormal and specific events for a fossil to materialize. Soon after a creature's death, a small or large catastrophe must take place near the deceased, which causes dirt to cover up the decedent quickly. Without rapid burial of the body, scavenging animals, bugs, and various erosional effects, including ultraviolet light, will destroy the animal prior to fossilization. Once the dirt buries the animal, fossilization can begin. That is, the minerals in the surrounding soil replace the soft tissue and bone marrow, hardening the object into a fossil.[1]

Paleontologists carefully unearth the fossil following intense and extensive documentation of the fossil location to include what items, rocks, strata, or other fossils are near the discovery. From this carefully executed removal, scientists can begin to grasp the history of the world, guess how the creature once lived, approximate when it died, its habitat, and various other pieces of knowledge. This data is not just to fill a scientist's personal journal but is an avenue by which mankind can begin to unravel our distant past. The question for this chapter is: "How distant is our past?"

INTRINSIC VERSUS EXTRINSIC

Debates between scientists about dinosaur extinction causation are a normal aspect of modern scientific literature. Some theories describe various asteroid strikes, an uncontrollable virus, cosmic radiation from an exploding supernova, and a variety of others.[2] While the theories diverge widely, there exist two primary schools of thought in which all theories reside. One is a slow process over an extensive period of time, known as intrinsic gradualists, while the other is extrinsic catastrophists or caused by a cataclysm.[3]

The intrinsic and extrinsic debate is similar in nature to the argument between scientists who are either uniformitarian evolutionists or catastrophic creationists. The creation-versus-evolution debate is primarily concerned with *how*, while dinosaur extinction studies focus on *when*. That is, nearly all Old-Earth evolutionists and/or creationists concur that roughly sixty-five million years ago, something in the world changed, leading to the mass extinction of virtually all large dinosaurs.

The dinosaur extinction occurs at what scientists have dubbed the K-T Boundary (some scientists now prefer the K-Pg Boundary or Cretaceous and Paleogene).[4] The *K* is short for Cretaceous (from the German word *Kreidezeit*), and the *T* represents Tertiary.[5] This boundary or extinction event also signifies a watershed moment in Earth's history from the Meso-zoic to the Cenozoic eras. Paleontologists continue to search for the answer as to what unknown factor drastically altered the earth's atmosphere to the point where large dinosaurs could no longer survive. We discern from the large deposits of fossils in the same strata all over the globe that either one major catastrophic event occurred or multiple localized events. Either way, something killed millions upon millions of animals while simultaneously triggering unique circumstances to take place, which allowed the extremely rare event of fossilization to mate-rialize all over the world.

In addition to the K-T event are the O-S, Late D, P-Tr, and Tr-J.[6] These extinction events are only the top five among hundreds of smaller recordings of mass extinctions.[7] The primary source for understanding each episode is marine animals, as they are more readily available in the fossil record.

The focus of this chapter is on the K-T boundary. The reader should keep in mind, however, that the K-T investigation is one of the hundreds of extinction events we could explore in which the extremely rare circumstances of fossilization transpired. That is, the exceptional occurrence needed to afford a creature deep (hungry scavengers will dig to uncover rotting carcasses) and immediate burial by moving wet dirt so fossilization can occur is repeated through each of the other hundreds of extinction records. Additionally, the hundreds of recorded extinction events with rapid burial and rare fossilization, oddly enough, occurred continuously around the world over and over again. When the logical conclusion of the evidence points in a different direction than what was first thought, that is the direction we must move. Neither one's opinion nor skepticism matters; it is the evidence that dictates. Is it possible something different transpired other than intrinsic or slow processes?

THE TIMELINE

Fossilized bones are just that and nothing more. While humorous to state, it is important to remember that bones do not come with a born-on date, expiration date, or family history to determine who their parents were, if they were parents (passed their genes to another generation), or if the location of death was their neighborhood.

Unlike operational science, which deals with observable and repeatable facts and makes computers, cell phones, and the like possible, historical scientists investigate evidence from the past and draw inferences from what they find. As previously mentioned, everyone has the same data; it is only our interpretation that varies, and one's presuppositions are what typically govern the conclusion.

COMPLEXITY

Darwinian evolution is a story of molecules to man, or simple to complex, of new life, odd creatures caught in incongruous stages with endless possibilities, and what exists today is just one of many potentialities. Without question, however, one of the most critical building blocks of this theory is the notion that every living organism evolved from simple singular-cellular life forms into the complex six-trillion-celled human being. The previous chapter quotes Darwin, the father of evolution, that without slow progression, his theory comes to an end.

Textbooks and teachers from elementary school through grad school inundate students with the so-called Evolutionary Tree of Life.[8] They proffer pictures of a tree trunk representing the simple life forms and crawl up the trunk and into the intricate branches of the complex life of today. The caption typically reads that life began as simple and slowly progressed via Darwinian evolutionary techniques such as natural selection to reach our current status.[9]

One problem with the Tree of Life, as proposed by evolutionists, is that little to no evidence exists to support its existence. I submit that after hundreds of years of paleontological digging all over the globe, findings substantiate the opposite. The Tree of Life looks like an upside-down tree, with the majority of complex life fully formed and fully functional at the start of the Cambrian Explosion and decreasing in number from that point. Many of these original creatures are now extinct, and the tree continues to dwindle as dozens of creatures go extinct every day with no new evolutionary advancements replacing them.[10]

Something to consider. We do not have organizations raising money to help relocate newly formed creatures as they evolve. In fact, we have the antithesis. Many non-profit groups exist to help stop the extinction of hundreds of species. Despite their best efforts, most of them end up extinct, never to return and, in many cases, man had nothing to do with their disappearance; they simply cannot survive. Nothing is popping into existence or evolving to replace them. It is simply a void, and extinction is our dilemma, not evolution/creation. The Tree of Life is standing on its branches, as animal life appears to be dying out.

Some would argue, at this point, that we do not live long enough to personally witness evolution. I understand that we do not live long enough to witness evolution *in its entirety*. We have lived long enough, however, to have witnessed pieces and parts of the process. That is, we should see millions of intermediaries, many of which should be grotesque monsters in the process of achieving completion, and most of them dying off due to their inability to endure as survival of the fittest, or more appropriately, natural selection rules the day. Said process is hoped for, yet only wishful thinking and imaginary.

According to the estimations by historical scientists — based on evolutionary theory — the beginning of life, or the trunk of the tree, contains single to multicellular microorganisms. Supposedly, these "simple" life forms evolved via natural selection into fish. The amount of transitional fossils necessary to arrive at such a staggering leap is unknown, but billions of them would be minimal.[11] Evolutionary biologists and paleontologists agree that there are necessarily more transitional creatures than fully formed and fully functional organisms or animals in their final stage.[12] One example is the fish-to-amphibian process, or eusthenopteron to ichthyostega. Considerable amounts of minuscule modifications need to take place for the eusthenopteron fish gills to reach the final operational stage of the ichthyostega lungs. Anything in between will either drown the fish or suffocate the amphib-

ian. Gills represent a small fraction of the total body transitions that need to transpire to eventually move an amoeba to a
fish.

The fossil record, therefore, should reveal a greater number
of transitional fossils as opposed to final stage animals. The
testimony of the fossils does not support said theory. A small
percentage of questionable transitional fossils exist (e.g.,
Archaeopteryx, Ichthyostega, et cetera), but out of the mass of
unearthed fossils over the last two centuries, a few questionable
transitions are all science possesses. Paleontologists have amoebas, and they have fish, but the hundreds of millions of years of
evolutionary evidence (transitionals) to arrive at a large-mouth
bass or a great white shark are absent. Almost every fossil we
locate is at the final stage of development, including the
amoeba. The idea of a Tree of Life is great except for one thing:
the evidence to substantiate the historical scientist's theory
about the trunk and branches is glaringly absent. There are
plenty of end-of-the-limb creatures, fully formed and fully
functional, but non-existent transitionals, except for a handful
that even evolutionists question the viability, to be called transitional.

Scientists will often use the term "missing link." This
phrase is misleading. They are not seeking a missing link; they
are diligently scouring the earth for missing links by the billions
—if not trillions. How amoebas became insects is conjecture
and wishful thinking. One evolutionist put it this way:

"When insect fossils first appear, in the Middle and Upper
Carboniferous, they are diverse and for the most part fully
winged. There are a few primitively wingless forms, but no
convincing intermediates are known. Reconstructing the "pro-
topterygotes" — the immediate ancestors of winged insects —

therefore relies, *as it always has, on indirect evidence.*"[13] (Emphasis mine)

Notice Wootton's use of the words: "indirect evidence." The only evidence they find is fully formed and fully functional creatures. Indirect evidence, therefore, is conjecture and wishful thinking. They believe natural selection took place because the empirical evidence they possess is final stage organisms, but no other system exists (without invoking special creation) to maneuver one creature to the next. Wootton and others are basically saying, "We observe the amoeba, and we see the insect; therefore, evolution must have transpired." Harvard professor George Wald stated it with intellectual honesty when he told the Scientific American Journal:

"One has only to contemplate the magnitude of this task to concede that the spontaneous generation of a living organism is impossible. Yet here we are — as a result, I believe, of spontaneous generation."[14]

If amoebas to insects were the only area where the fossil record was lacking, one might be remiss in calling an entire theory into question. The facts remain, however, that missing links exist in every GC strata layer and in every known fossilized or living creature. When searching for links between fish and frogs, salamanders and caecilians, Carroll wrote, "...We have found no fossil evidence of any possible antecedents that possessed the specialized features common to all three modern orders."[15] When seeking intermediates from snakes to lizards, Colbert wrote, "Unfortunately, the fossil history of the snake is very fragmentary, so that it is necessary to infer much of their evolution."[16] Or, as paleontologists attempt to locate fossil evidence to help support the evolutionary belief that birds emerged from reptiles, Swinton wrote, "The origin of birds is largely a matter of deduction. There is no fossil evidence of the stages through which the remarkable change from reptile to bird was achieved."[17]

This list continues from one creature to the next, and the quotes are similar from those who are willing to be intellectually honest in their journals. The transitional fossils evolutionists desire appear to be nonexistent. This statement is true considering that after nearly two hundred years of well-funded and widely-spread excavating, a few questionable fossils are as good as it gets.

MICRO VERSUS MACRO

As previously mentioned, all scientists have the same data; the only difference is the interpretation of said data. Some, depending on their worldview and presuppositions, will view one piece of evidence as supporting their belief system, while other scientists in the same field will see it as buttressing their opposing convictions. Microevolution and macroevolution are prime examples of said discussion.

No serious scientist or researcher denies that organisms have the ability to adapt to their surroundings. The genome and epigenome have this amazing possibility built into each cell, which is readily observable, verifiable, and repeatable. A beetle, moth, or lizard, for example, can alter the color of its body in one generation to better conceal itself from predators. A bird's DNA can turn on or off specific areas to increase or decrease the length of its beak based on what the environmental conditions mandate. And human genome allows for variations of melanin to account for the amount of ultraviolet light they are receiving to protect the body from damage.[18] The list of minor alterations, known as either microevolution or adaptations, is extensive and readily prevalent.[19]

There is, however, a vast difference between a creature adapting to its surroundings yet remaining the same creature, and, for instance, when an amoeba becomes a fish, a lizard becomes a bird, or a chimpanzee becomes a Homo erectus or Neanderthal and eventually modern man. That is, a moth with different colored wings is still a moth, a shortened beak on a finch is still a finch, and a dog with a thicker coat is still a dog. None of these adaptations add any significant alterations that maneuver said animal toward becoming another animal.[20]

Additionally, when conditions return to how the animal is accustomed to living, the genes typically return the animal to its starting point. In other words, evidence supports the idea that built into the genome is the ability to adapt or create a variation of the same creature to assist in its survival. Even more miraculous is the autocorrect mechanism of the epigenome as it ordinarily returns the creature and obtains biological homeostasis. For example, scientists estimate that ultraviolet light damages nearly every cell in our body roughly one million times a day.[21] The amazing aspect is the cell has the ability to return the damaged parts of the cell to their original healthy state within one generation or cellular mitosis. If the cell is beyond repair, it recognizes its mutated stage and enters a self-destruct phase or apoptosis.[22] Cells, not the brain, somehow have the ability to recognize repairable damage and harm beyond restoration and respond appropriately.

Macroevolution states that one creature, given enough time and appropriate conditions, becomes an entirely different creature. A major hurdle, however, is that it is not observable, verifiable, or repeatable. Unfortunately, good scientists use poor decisions to draw comparisons between operational science (micro) and historical science (macro). Ultimately, when one makes a connection between microevolution and macroevolution, it is nothing more than conjecture; they make an unscientific blind leap of faith.[23]

CONCLUSION

This chapter does not call a given scientist's intellect into question, not at all; they are often brilliant individuals. What I am stating is a known epistemological imperative; one's grasp of the world colors their interpretation. We, therefore, as intellectual beings, have every right, if not obligation, to humbly question data, rationally think through the evidence, and logically decipher the conclusions of experts in the field. It is no different from when a parent, teacher, or pastor makes a claim to truth. If one cannot verify said assertion for veracity, then one should call the supposition into question.

While this topic is an ongoing debate, the fossil record does not support the idea of macroevolution. In fact, the fossil record continues to demonstrate the exact opposite. According to empirical data from millions of unearthed fossils, the preponderance of evidence simply does not support the preconceived notion held by evolutionists of molecules to man. Strata after strata reveal a sudden or rapid appearance of life followed, not by increasing complexity, but by massive amounts of extinctions. Said extinctions are continuing today with no evolutionary new creatures coming into existence. In other words, the observable and testable data points the scientist toward a creationist's theory. Evolutionary theory is nearly exclusively dependent on conjecture from historical and unsupported scientific data.

In a court of law, this debate is heavily weighted in favor of the creationist. At the end of the trial, the jury could take with them to the deliberation room the physical evidence of the

Cambrian Explosion, geneticists' proof of mutation correction devices, adaptations that go nowhere except assisting a creature to survive, and millions of fossils containing the four *F-words* of evolution: fully formed, fully functional. A bird with teeth or claws is hardly admissible in that some birds we view today have teeth and claws used to survive, not evolve. There was no addition or deletion in the genome, only the ability to better survive in its environment. It is not on its way to becoming another animal.

CHAPTER 5

THE GRAND CANYON

I WILL NEVER FORGET the first time I stood at the South Rim of the Grand Canyon. I was twelve years old, and it was the most magnificent and breathtaking moment of my short life. I have since had the opportunity to revisit this marvel of the natural world multiple times, and I have yet to become accustomed to its majesty. Its beauty is beyond eloquent words, and its magnitude transcends photography. And the words that are on everyone's lips when viewing its grandeur are often, "How was this made?"

One of the most powerful natural forces effectuating environmental change is water. Given enough time, even a small trickle erodes solid rock and turns steel into dust. Water in high volumes reorganizes entire landscapes, recreates streambeds, and obliterates anything in its path. The remnants of water damage cover the face of the globe.

In the powerful 8.9 earthquake off the coast of Japan in early 2011, humankind witnessed the unimaginable force of massive amounts of displaced water. In a few short hours, the face of Japan's landscape forever changed, and natural and manmade barriers did almost nothing to impede its flow. The might of water is something we are just beginning to understand, and its scars are everywhere.

A prevalent evidence of water's movement is the innumerable riverbed carvings. Many are only a few inches deep, while others, like the Channeled Scablands of Washington and Linville Gorge in North Carolina, are sculpted valleys of beauty. There is one chasm that dwarfs them all in notoriety and most of them in size: the Grand Canyon (GRC). Geologists continue to spend untold thousands of man-hours researching the strata of this unique area of exposed time. No one disputes the fact that water is primarily responsible for carving the winding path of the GRC. There is a difference of opinion, however, as to whether its creation was due to a rapid catastrophe or a slow uniformitarian process. Once again, everyone has the same dumb and mute evidence; it is the observer who must interpret.

SIX QUESTIONS

Walt Brown proposed the GRC formed rapidly via a catastrophic event occurring roughly four to five hundred years after the Noetic Flood. He theorizes two massive lakes, Grand and Hopi Lakes, remnants of the flood, suddenly drained when their earthen dams broke.[1] He proposed twenty-four questions based on geographical features in and around the GRC, for which geologists must provide answers in order to arrive at a conclusion of uniformitarianism or catastrophism: (1) Layering; (2) Limestone; (3) Marble Canyon; (4) Distant Cavern Connections; (5) Side Canyons; (6) Barbed Canyons; (7) Slot Canyons; (8) Perpendicular Faults; (9) Arching; (10) Inner Gorge; (11) Nankoweap Canyon; (12) Unusual Erosion; (13) Forces, Energy, and Mechanism; (14) Why Here; (15) Why so Recently; (16)

Missing River; (17) Missing Talus; (18) Kaibab Plateau; (19) Colorado River; (20) Missing Mesozoic Rock; (21) Missing Dirt; (22) Fossils; (23) Tipped Layers; (24) Time or Intensity.[2]

This project covers six of Brown's twenty-four questions:

First, how did such a relatively small river create such a massive trench? The gorge is an incredible earthly gouge measuring two hundred seventy-seven miles long, at least eighteen miles wide, averaging four thousand feet deep, and over one million acres of land. When one views it from thirty thousand feet, the Colorado River does not appear to have the mass to account for the sprawling canyons of the GRC.

The geological evidence demonstrates that this land, at least since the creation of the GRC, has been arid. The National Park Service lists the GRC as one of the few arid land erosions.[3] This does not appear to disturb uniformitarians, but it should, given the amount of water it would take to carve the canyon does not show evidence of its existence at the park or surrounding landscape. The typical additional forms of erosion, e.g., wind, freeze and thaw, rain, et cetera, are also accepted, but the relatively small Colorado River remains the primary source. The river was once much larger prior to man tapping into its resources. Even at its peak, however, we will still need to suspend our current geologic understanding in order to believe it is responsible for such widespread erosion.

Side-barbed canyons are also evidence of a local catastrophe. It is unusual to find barbed canyons around rivers or streams, as tributaries typically connect at right or acute angles. They are, however, normal in flood plains, where the water rushes against gravity due to topography and swiftly back to the low point prior to following the natural flow of the slope of the land.[4] It would be like sloshing water around in a water basin. The water would run up the sidewalls because of the force of the movement. A second later, gravity takes over, and the water returns to the lowest part of the basin. On a large scale, such movement would leave erosion evidence that appears to defy logic unless one considers a flood scenario.

A second hesitation is the sharp, parallel, and multicolored strata lines known as layering. As one stands on the rim of the GRC, it is difficult to miss the incredibly stark symmetrical strata lines. These multicolored lines do not stop as one cliff ends and another begins hundreds of yards and sometimes miles away. The color and geological makeup do not alter. There is no problem with this reality if the GRC's strata were laid down rapidly and then eroded later, but that is not what uniformitarians submit. They state the stratum built up over tens of millions of years and eroded slowly. If this is true, micro-climates would have left evidence via distinctive erosional patterns in the strata lines. That is, small stream runoff creates downcutting forces, creating broken strata lines across miles of visible layers. For example, we commonly witness flooding in one location while other areas receive no rain at all. It is common for visitors to look out from the North Rim and view a snowstorm or rainstorm covering the western half of the GRC while the sun is bright and shining on the eastern half. The runoff will be unequal from these events and, therefore, leave variant erosional features from one peak to the next. If one walks along the top layer of the GRC, the soil records this common weather occurrence. There is evidence of erosion of multiple variations on the top layer, but not within the strata lines exposed thousands of feet down and over many square miles. The geologic evidence lends itself to a rapid layering of the strata, not a slow build-up over time, as uniformitarians require.

The third issue is that out of all the land in the world, why did the GRC form in its location? The Colorado River is 1,450 miles long, and only nineteen percent is the GRC, despite similar geology. If the river etched the GRC, why does it suddenly start near Marble Canyon and stop its amazing erosion at mile two hundred seventy-seven at the Grand Wash Cliffs? There is no known mechanism or reason for the GRC to stop where it does. This sudden stop lends itself to a local catastrophic event, such as a dam break that lost its incredible force after a few hundred miles of dispersing over the land.

Why a gorge begins and ends is typically easy to decipher. For instance, the topography where the Linville River in North Carolina flows through is a steep descent until it levels out and pours into Lake James. As the water swiftly makes its way to the lowest gravitational pull, it carves Linville Gorge. In other words, the impetus is a large volume of water over steep terrain that is at a sharper gradient than the area above the gorge, ending when the land levels out. This is not the case at GRC, as the general topography is roughly the same before and after the GRC.

There are gorges that go deeper, some are wider, and a few are longer, but none compare to the grandeur of the GRC; there is a reason it is one of the seven natural wonders of the world. Most rivers of much greater flow volume than the Colorado River do not even begin to carve out their beds like the GRC. The Amazon is a long and bending river basin, the Mississippi is much longer with an incredible flow rate and plenty of opportunities to create canyons, but there is nothing resembling the GRC on either river. The list is practically endless: the Rogue River in Oregon, the Yuba River in California, the Delaware River in New York and Pennsylvania, the Niobrara River in Nebraska, and many other high-volume rivers, but no great canyons.

The Grand Canyon is unique for many reasons, but the most obvious is that it exists where it does. Many other rivers of the world have similar riverbed geology and surrounding geological features, yet are devoid of the incredible cuts found in the GRC.

A fourth point of contention is large-scale volumes of missing mountain talus. Talus forms at the base of mountains due to the effects of erosion and the law of gravity. The dirt and rocks simply move from a high point to a low point. Old, steep mountains become a pile of rubble given enough time. During this slow process, fallen debris litters the base of the mountain, creating a sloped pile that geologists call talus.

While there are piles of talus at the base of some of the cliff faces in the GRC, they are either too small, given the size of the landscape, or non-existent.[5] Of particular interest is the entrance to the GRC, Marble Canyon, which has almost no talus. Scientists are aware of this anomaly but give credit to high-volume floods that sweep the canyon and thereby take with it the talus.[6] If this issue was only in places that correlate with uniformitarians' proposal of flood removal, that might be a good explanation. There are, however, a few problems with this theory.

The area is unarguably accepted as arid, and there is no evidence of large-scale floods occurring in the barbed canyons and other relatively flat desert plains between cliffs.[7]

The low flat plain areas are also without the amounts of

talus that should exist with no known method of removal, as water does not flow through them at any rate other than rain and snow runoff.

Additionally, a sizeable region of missing talus is in the Vermilion and Echo Cliffs sections in the northern area of the park. This is a problem for uniformitarians, as these cliffs consist of softer lower-level strata with heavier and stronger upper strata.[8] This type of scenario should lead to large piles of heavy rock talus as the older, softer rock crumbles under the pressure of the strata above. While there are piles, these mounds are too small to account for hundreds of thousands of years of erosion, possibly thousands, but not hundreds of thousands.[9]

A fifth inquiry that does not appear to support long-period uniformitarianism is the missing dirt from the erosion runoff; the Colorado River delta is too small. A delta forms when sediment from a riverbed moves from the river and enters a lake or ocean. As the flow of the river succumbs to the stationary lake or ocean, the sediment settles to the bottom, causing a delta of river deposits.[10] For example, the Mississippi River Delta is choking off of the Gulf of Mexico entrance. From this expected occurrence, New Orleans is taking on water from this natural land dam.

The Colorado River Delta is located in the Gulf of California. Due to the many dams and siphoning of the Colorado, the flow of the fifteen-million-acre feet of annual water into the Gulf has been reduced to ten percent of the original.[11] At one time, the Colorado was moving five hundred thousand tons of debris a day and transporting it to the Gulf.[12] This massive movement of material has stopped due to damming and city and farm usage of the river. Over the last eighty years since the dams began, ninety percent of the once sprawling two-million-acre delta has vanished.[13] There is no longer enough force to move the sediments out to sea, and the once thriving estuary lies nearly dormant.

Even with this massive amount of sediment movement leading to an incredible delta, there is still not enough dirt to account for the amount of material removed from the GRC area, not to mention the entire Colorado River basin. Geologists estimate the total volume of rock, dirt, and sand the Colorado River had to excavate and transport downstream at eight hundred cubic miles.[14] When one takes into account the missing top layer of Mesozoic dirt of at least four thousand feet, with estimates as high as ten thousand feet prior to any carving into the top layer of limestone of the GRC, one must add between sixteen and twenty-five thousand cubic miles of additional material to the equation (this missing dirt is what gives the GRC the flat tabletop).[15] The amount of missing dirt is astounding. At the delta's peak, there was only one percent of the volume of the GRC dirt.[16] Again, and critical to this investigation, this does not take into account the stripped-away top layer of Mesozoic strata ranging in depth from four to ten thousand feet.[17] If one were to add this material into the equation, the amount would be far less than one percent of debris. Where is all the dirt? Consider this: eight hundred cubic miles is roughly equal to all the water in all the rivers and streams in the entire world and multiplying that amount times two. Again, this amount includes neither the missing Mesozoic layer (25,000 cubic miles, or three times that of the GRC) nor the deep canyons before and after the GRC; this is only the GRC itself, and we have one percent or less in the delta. The evidence appears to be pointing in a different direction, namely, a large, rapid force pushing that inconceivable amount of dirt and rock much further.

A relatively slow and long-term uniformitarian approach to this problem does not solve the issue. The dirt is simply not where it should exist; it is gone. Conversely, a catastrophic event such as a massive land dam break causing a large flood does fit the evidence. A flood would have enough force to spread the debris across the land mass just west of the GRC, where the Grand Wash Cliffs mark the end of this unique feature. There would be enough force to drive the material until it reached the Gulf, where it would be transported far into the Gulf with little delta remaining. It would be a type of intense pressure washing of the delta, clearing it of years of buildup.

The sixth question is the most captivating and involves the Kaibab Plateau (KP). Of all geologic studies conducted over the years, geologists appear to struggle more over the existence of the KP than the existence of the GRC. One finds the problem that causes this stir in elementary physics; water does not run uphill. The Colorado River enters the GRC at 3100 feet above sea level, and standing in the way is the elevated KP, which is nearly six thousand feet above the Colorado River.[18] Because water cannot naturally run uphill, yet the Colorado River cuts through the KP, there must be an explanation given for this apparent scientific discrepancy.

Long-age uniformitarian scientists describe varying events occurring many millions of years ago. They speculate about extinct rivers and lakes; the problem is they do not have a foundation in the geologic record. The only known evidence is the reality that the KP exists and the Colorado River cuts through it. When one holds ardently to uniformitarian principles in GRC formation, normal geological explanations do not work, and we must turn to unlikely, if not illogical, possibilities.

One prominent theory to explain this anomaly is an ancient lake they call Bidahochi. This lake was supposedly formed when an "ancestral" river (there is no geological evidence for the river) flowed above the KP, heading the opposite way (east) of the current flow of the Colorado. The KP would not allow the lake to drain, so, in time, a river formed to the south of the KP. As the river flowed for a while, it eventually caused a breach in the KP, opening it up for the ancestral river to begin to flow through the KP (river capture), and the GRC came into existence over a five-million-year expanse.[19]

The aforementioned story is largely speculation based on little more than a need to create a reason for water cutting through a higher elevated plateau. Some Bidahochi theorists admit this truth and openly write about the lack of evidence for said lake's existence.[20] Further, the six concerns listed in this report are not a surprise to most uniformitarian geologists, and some openly recognize the barriers they create and the direction their answers point: catastrophism. These individuals understand these issues, attempt to solve them, and due to the overwhelming evidence, are leaning toward a catastrophic event. This does not mean they admit the Noetic Flood led to the creation of the GRC, but it alludes to a catastrophic event in lieu of a long, slow process.

Two geologists wrote:

"...Lake-overflow hypothesis might help to explain rapid incision of the Grand Canyon. It also fits with the downstream sedimentary record, and it could explain the lack of evidence for a major lake upstream of the Grand Canyon in the latest Miocene and Pliocene epochs. Finally, the overflow hypothesis does not require any late Cenozoic uplift of the Colorado Plateau to explain incision within and upstream of the Grand

Canyon because rapid dissection is a consequence of over-flowing drainage reaching a much lower base level."[21]

Meek and Douglas are not Young-Earth creationists but remain intellectually honest and follow the evidence found in the GRC. They recognize multiple features of the GRC that point to a catastrophe and are attempting to understand by what means such an event or events occurred. Their first question is how "rapid incision" occurred. This type of geologic feature occurs during floods as the water rapidly flows over and/or recedes from a high point to a low point, as witnessed in multiple floods such as the Indonesian tsunami of 2004. Secondly, downstream sedimentary record; in other words, the delta is too small for the large volume of material that once filled the GRC. Thirdly, they want to know why there is a lack of evidence for a major lake. These geologists find zero evidence to support the popularly held belief of Lake Bida-hochi. Fourthly, and most telling, they recognize the logical problems associated with the KP uplift occurring at a later time rather than earlier when they wrote, "[the KP]...does not require any late Cenozoic uplift of the Colorado Plateau."[22]

GRAND CANYON FORMATION THEORY

Dr. Walter Brown provides a detailed theory as to the creation of the GRC in his book *In the Beginning*.[23] Brown explains the geological evidence found in the GRC and delta in the following manner.

Rapidly laid strata layers of the GRC formed during the yearlong Noetic Flood event. According to the Bible and other writings from variant culture groups, a large volume of water covered the earth for an extended period of time, likely over a year.[24] As the waters slowly receded to their gravitational low points, many high-elevation lakes formed, held only by natural land dams. Two of the largest lakes in the world developed just north and east of where the GRC exists today; the Grand Lake to the north and Hopi Lake to the east. The Grand Lake extended through North West Arizona and into South East Utah, Western Colorado, and North West New Mexico. Hopi Lake's waters extended from the GRC to the New Mexico border. Two earthen dams just north of the GRC held these massive lakes at bay.

Within four to five hundred years of the Noetic Flood, while the GRC sediments were still wet and pliable, the waters of the Grand Lake breached its dam. The large volume of water began to carve the Vermillion and Echo Cliffs. These features signify the entrance of the Colorado River into the GRC. As the waters continued their flow southward, they breached the second land dam, confining the waters of the Hopi Lake. The dam rapidly eroded as the water flowed, causing it to begin to cascade toward the soft sediment to the south. As this considerable volume of water scoured the land in its path, it took the Mesozoic top layer of the GRC with it, giving the entire region the familiar tabletop appearance. Additionally, as the weight of the Mesozoic layer moved, the counterweight of the Grand and Hopi Lakes and Colorado Plateau began to upthrust the soft KP strata, driving it skyward several thousand feet in a matter of hours, not thousands of years (Google "Pakistan Earthquake" to get a modern visual). The Colorado and Little Colorado Rivers were already carving away their river bottom. Water did not run uphill; the hill arose shortly after the water began its course.[25]

Besides the cliffs and KP creation, several other prominent features formed. One of those is the Nankoweap Canyon. The Nankoweap came into existence primarily from the backwash of both rivers as the KP rose out of the ground, creating a barrier for the massive amounts of flowing water. The Little

Colorado River shot its waters at this monolith like a shotgun but could not overcome the height of the KP, so it took the debris down the now-forming GRC, scouring everything in its path.

The barbed canyons surrounding the Vermillion and Echo Cliffs formed as the waters flowed away from the rising KP and into the lower elevation of the Colorado River. Slumping (large singular mass of earth movement) of some of these canyons is present due to the water saturation of the strata.[26] As the waters receded, many of these slot canyons began to slump as the intense water pressure exited the sand, pushing the soil out in the process. This is why many of these canyons give the appearance of water formation but lack two things: (1) enough water in an arid location and 2) gravitational slope. That is, water should not flow from the Colorado River uphill (south) to a dead end. If these canyons had exit points at their ends, slumping would not be an issue. However, because they abruptly terminate, slumping has become a predominant feature.

The dozens of cubic miles of excavated debris flowed downstream at a high velocity. Brown believes the missing dirt of both the four- to ten-thousand-foot Mesozoic layer (sixteen to twenty-five cubic miles) and the GRC volume (eight hundred cubic miles) are not in the Colorado River delta. The waters pushed the sediment out to sea, creating the land masses we recognize today: the Imperial Sand Dunes of California and the northern part of the Baja of California.[27] Unlike the slow processes that create deltas, this water and sediment were moving as if a flood rushing to its lowest level with no barriers, and the delta formed following this catastrophic event.

CONCLUSION

The geologic evidence is so overwhelming that some uniformitarians contrive stories with no corroborating evidence to support their belief. They use terms that lead to one's imagination running wild, with little to no hydraulic or geologic mechanisms taken into account. Anyone can invent hopes based on their presuppositions, but supplying the required evidence and applying the geologic mechanisms is another story.

I believe, based on the preponderance of evidence, that the GRC formed in a matter of roughly one week, not millions of years. The rocks cry out the truth of this event. The geology fits the unlikely yet accurate hypothesis of a catastrophic event. Similar to the Channel Scablands of Washington state, the only real issue for the uniformitarian is from where the water originated?[28] As mentioned, serious scientists believe that at one time, frozen water covered most of the earth.[29] The problem apparently only causes concern when it is in a liquid state. I believe the difficulty is not that large volumes of water obviously carved the GRC; the problem is that such an event supports the events as the Bible records in the Noetic Flood. The challenge is not in the corroborating proofs but in one's worldview.

At best, this chapter is a cursory study of the material, but all the chapters in this series are intended to ignite a desire in the reader to seek out further information. The Grand Canyon is truly a marvel, but its creation is even more intriguing, and the chance to understand this enigma is mesmerizing.

CHAPTER 6

RADIOMETRIC DATING

ONE OF THE most persuasive yet fiercely debated techniques that scientists use to date objects is radiometric dating. It seems that at least once a week, one will read a headline similar to the following from ABC News, "Scientists accurately date the earliest human fossil." The subtitle reads, "Arguably the most accurate dates ever achieved for early human fossils."[1] The two natural questions that arise out of such a caption are: What made the change necessary if radiometric dating methods are accurate? And how do they know it is arguably accurate this time — what about next year?

Further, in this news article, the author used the word new. New indicates a change. That alteration is the age of Australopithecus Afarensis (commonly known as Lucy). Radiometric dating machines estimate Lucy's original age at 3.2 million years.[2] This new date places her at only 1.98 million, give or take 3,000 years. That is a 1.22-million-year variance from the first time that scientists placed her bones in the machine.

The specific methods used were uranium-lead and paleomagnetic analysis. Experts have great difficulty determining how old a piece of furniture or painting is from just a few thousand years ago, so it seems appropriate to call into question the validity of such a bold statement as 1.98 million years, give or take 3,000. One cannot forget that neither Lucy nor any other object we discover from ancient history has a date stamp. The date is a mystery, and the processes to determine age are far from precise.

Consider this new reading of the evidence and compare it to something tangible for most of us. Imagine receiving a speeding ticket for driving sixty-five miles per hour in a fifty-five-mile-per-hour zone. You take the ticket to court, and when the judge asks the officer if anything has changed since she wrote the ticket, she responds with, "Yes, I have recalculated the defendant's speed and determined he was actually going thirty-five miles per hour, give or take three miles per hour." Or worse, "I have thought about it, your honor, and I am not sure the radar gun was accurate, but let's go with that because that's all I have." Would the court throw out the ticket or permit such discrepancies and allow the ticket to stand? Either the machine is accurate based on human input/error, or it is flawed due to human input/error. That is, similar to a radar gun, the machine is only as accurate as the data a human entered into its processor. If the data is flawed, the results will be flawed.

IS THE MACHINE TRUSTWORTHY?

Depending on the latest article or peer-reviewed publication one reads, the debate over the accuracy and reliability of radiometric dating methods (RDM) is not over. The discussion is highly technical, with untold and currently unknowable quantities such as evaporation rates, parent-to-daughter-decay rates, and various other fluctuations. The spectrum of possibilities about this argument is a work in progress. Reaching a final consensus is unlikely on this side of Heaven.

Both sides (i.e., Young-Earth and Old-Earth scientists) make assumptions to arrive at their given solution. These assumed quantities have the potential to debunk or, at a minimum, call into question the premise and conclusions of the argument. Both admit and use said suppositions against each other's arguments. One must, therefore, weigh the best evidence possible and formulate an opinion on this aggressive and expansive topic. One cannot, however, appeal to popularity to formulate a conclusion; ultimate reality and truth are the keys.

THE BASICS OF RADIOMETRIC DATING METHODS

Atoms are the basic building blocks of matter and life. Most atoms are in a stable state and do not alter given normal situations. There are, however, some atoms that are unstable. An unstable atom is in a state of flux, moving from a heavy atom to a lighter one.[3] These volatile atoms are radioactive and emit large amounts of energy that are often harmful to living organisms.

The original unstable stage of a nuclear atom is the parent element. As the parent loses or emits an isotope from its nucleus, it enters a stable or resting phase, known as the daughter element. The time it takes for an unstable element to become a stable element, known as the decay rate or half-life, is represented as $t \frac{1}{2}$. Scientists are able to witness via empirical tests the $t \frac{1}{2}$ of nuclear atoms. These known times vary from one radioactive element to another. Some are brief: polonium 215 $t\frac{1}{2}$ is 0.0018 seconds. Others take a long time: uranium 238 $t \frac{1}{2}$ is 4.5 billion years.[4]

The following is a short list of nuclear and/or unstable

elements commonly used by scientists to attempt to date the Earth. The first element is the unstable parent, and the second one is the stable and resting daughter element. The number after the daughter is the believed half-life.[5]

Table 1. Radioactive Half-Life
  Parent Isotope
  Stable Daughter Product
  Currently Accepted Half-Life
  Uranium-238
  Lead-206
  4.5 billion years
  Uranium-235
  Lead-207
  704 million years
  Thorium-232
  Lead-208
  14 billion years

ASSUMPTIONS

One of the most critical aspects of RDM is the original amount of parent-to-daughter ratio. If scientists cannot determine the original amount, there is no way to conclude how long the element has been decaying. The only thing one can test is how quickly the element is currently decaying.

Scientists center their age findings on assumptions based on extrapolations from currently known values. This does not negate the strong possibility of wide fluctuations of radiometric decay over time. One can guess, but cannot know, the original amount in a given product.

A well-known example is if a man walks into a room and a

candle is burning, he can know a few things: (1) The candle was lit at some point. (2) The burn rate of the candle. (3) How tall the candle is currently. (4) The time it will take for the candle to burn out. What he cannot know is how tall the candle was when it was lit.[6] In the case of the decay rate of uranium 238 (U-238), no living organism existed 4.5 billion years ago to establish a known beginning quantity. Given the amount of daughter element we verify today, at best, one can extrapolate backward to attempt to determine the original amount of parent U-238 in a given sample, but it is without certainty.

RADIOCARBON DATING METHOD

A popular method of dating recent items (relatively speaking) is radiocarbon dating (RCD) or carbon-fourteen dating. It is common to hear experts on a variety of educational channels use this dating method for items made by humankind and/or hominids. For example, the dating method has been used on cave pottery, the Dead Sea Scrolls, the Shroud of Turin, and various other organic materials made from an organism recovered in archeological finds around the globe. RCD is a feasible means of dating most ancient objects since plant and animal life were the common bases.

Similar to RMD, RCD relies on known starting quantities of an unstable parent element moving to a stable daughter element. The products in question are various stages of carbon: carbon 14 (14C), carbon 13 (13C), and carbon 12 (12C). The unstable parent carbon is 14C, degenerating into the stable daughter element nitrogen 14 (14N). The t ½ of 14C is 5,730 years.[7] The amount of carbon available in the carbon reservoir is broken down into roughly 98.89% 12C, 1.11% 13C, and 0.0000000010% 14C.[8]

CREATION OF 14C

Bombarding the earth's upper atmosphere is radiation, primarily from the sun and secondarily from distant stars deeper in outer space. The upper atmosphere, or stratosphere, is largely (78%) nitrogen-14 (14N). The atomic compound for 14N is seven protons and seven neutrons.[9] Occasionally, radiation strikes 14N at a precise angle, knocking a proton out, thereby allowing an additional neutron to attach to the nitrogen. This change alters the compound from a stable seven protons and seven neutrons to an unstable six protons and eight neutrons, or a 14C.[10]

As radiation creates 14C across the sky, the radioactive particles descend to earth and sporadically react with oxygen atoms, creating unstable carbon dioxide.[11] Living plants readily absorb and use carbon dioxide to grow and thrive. Vegetation acts as an air scrubber, cleaning the air of deadly carbon dioxide. Plants have an amazing ability to somehow distinguish between stable 12C and unstable 14C and absorb them at different rates.

Scientists believe they know the rate of said discrimination and consider it as nominal and attempt to compensate for said minor discrepancies via 13C comparisons.[12] Plants simply absorb carbon at given saturation rates as found in their habitats. As the plant grows, it rapidly reaches a point of equilibrium congruent with its environment. A plant, therefore, contains an equal amount of 14C and 12C that surrounds the plant. Scientists call the known amounts of 14C and 12C the carbon exchange reservoir.[13]

Said differently, a plant cannot contain more than 14C or 12C than what the atmosphere offers. The carbon amount in the plant is equal to the carbon amount outside the plant, despite plant absorption discrimination. For all intents and purposes, they are equal. For example, water locks work off of this principle. The one side begins with more water than the other side. The operator opens a valve to allow the water to flow into the other lower lock. This flow continues until both locks have equalized, and the boat can move from one to the other. No pumps are required for this event, just opening a valve and allowing water to reach equilibrium.

Reaching equilibrium in the carbon exchange reservoir is a significant aspect of RCD. As one can imagine, if the available carbon amounts fluctuate, one cannot determine how much original 14C was in the plant at death. At the point of death, the plant, for the most part, does not absorb any more carbon. The 14C t ½ clock of 5,730 years begins to tick at the moment of death. The parent 14C slowly returns to the daughter 14N, and as the nitrogen reenters the atmosphere, it has the potential to begin the cycle again.[14] I need to reinforce a key to this process: dead plants and dead creatures cannot absorb carbon (minus an insignificant amount or contamination), but carbon does exit the decaying item and return to the atmosphere.

While animals and humans do not readily absorb 14C as a plant does, they do eat plants containing the unstable element. As the food is processed, the ingesting body absorbs the 14C from the plants and stores it in the bones.[15] Animal and/or human bones, therefore, can be carbon dated just as a product made from plant life (e.g., It was common to use plants to add strength to pottery, and most clothing derives from plant and animal life. These items, therefore, can be carbon dated).

The reader cannot miss this next point due to its indispens-able nature of evidence relevance: each of the parent elements can only go through so many t ½ before the product is unde-tectable by current technology. That is, given the low amount of 14C, even at its peak, it does not take many t ½ lives to reach a point of being undetectable. While there is some debate, the range of time that scientists can detect 14C in a product is from 50,000 (roughly nine half-lives) to 100,000 years (nearly seventeen half-lives).[16] A product older than 100,000 years should not and cannot, therefore, have any detectable 14C remaining.[17]

To miss this point is as perilous as interrogating a suspect who gives conflicting and thereby, paradoxical statements, never recognizing his misstep. For the record, at the most extreme and liberal end of the 14C spectrum, there is no argument that no item older than 100,000 years can possibly contain detectable 14C (I cover cross-contamination, but said issue raises even more concerns for this researcher). The suspect was either near the crime scene or he was miles away; he cannot be at both locations. Either the 14C has decayed and shifted back into the atmosphere, or it remains at the scene of death.

HOW RCD DETERMINES AGE

Scientists remove a small sample of a given product so they can test it for its 14C to 12C ratio. They burn the sample in a controlled environment, and as the captured smoke leaves the product, a Geiger counter determines the amount of radioactive 14C in the product. They compare the ratio of 14C to 12C that was in the product to known ratios in the carbon exchange reservoir, which then gives the scientists an approximate age.[18]

RCD DIFFICULTIES

First, there are problems in determining atmospheric equilibrium.[19] An imperative aspect of this testing is the ratio of 14C to 12C in the atmosphere or carbon reservoir. If there are changes or fluctuations in the amount of available 14C through the centuries, then it becomes difficult to impossible to obtain an accurate reading of a given product. Some scientists put the 14C fluctuation at ten percent variances.[20]

For example, studies of the atmosphere over the last century provide clear evidence that the available amount of 14C does alter greatly.[21] The amount of volcanism, magnetic strength, solar radiation, nuclear bomb testing, and other factors, known and unknown, directly affect the available amount of 14C for photosynthesis, and these are just some of the known problems. As always, what we don't know is potentially just as detrimental, if not worse.

This type of research indicates that what scientists perceive as equilibrium, in actuality, has the ability to alter from year to year. Scientists attempt to overcome said dilemma by using tree and ice ring dating methods. Researchers call this technique cross-dating.[22] They assert that by studying tree rings, one can better determine the available 14C reservoir at the time of the given product's lifespan. Given this approximation, they can closely estimate the age of said product.

Since the most critical aspect of 14C is unreliable, then the whole process should logically be called into question. For instance, it is empirically known that the twentieth century has had large fluctuations of 14C; thus, the identical possibility for previous centuries is unlikely or, at best, minimally possible. Conversely, if the 14C decay rate is constant and unchanging in the atmosphere upon reaching equilibrium, then why, given billions of years, is our atmosphere not at equilibrium?[23]

Second, scientists have shown that plants discriminate against heavier atoms of carbon in their uptake and use.[24] Hence, even if 14C to 12C reaches equilibrium in the carbon reservoir, certain plants choose the lighter 12C over the heavier 14C. The problem this presents to the test is a skewed ratio of 12C to 14C. The product will give a false reading of greater age because there is less 14C than was present in the reservoir at the time the plant was alive. Scientists refer to this problem as fractionation.[25] Scientists attempt to compensate for fractionation via what they know. That is, what is commonly found is a specific percent difference between the ratio of 13C to 12C and a doubling of that number between 13C and 14C, as far as they can tell.[26]

Third, since Willard Libby and his colleagues discovered 14C dating methods in 1949, scientists have tried and failed to locate a measurable substance (e.g., organic materials made from an organism) with zero 14C.[27]

For example, coal, considered to be several hundred million years old, should not have a trace of 14C remaining, but it does.[28] Other ancient plant material that should have long ago moved from the unstable parent 14C to the stable daughter element, 14N, contains some amount of 14C.[29]

Scientists continue to try to zero or procedurally blank the accelerator mass spectrometer with a vegetation product, but to no avail. There are some trace amounts of 14C, and they cannot blank the machine. Some researchers decry that, while this is true, the problems stem from cross-contamination from other radioactive rocks that surround the product or poor or unknown problems in the dating method.[30]

Going back to the speeding ticket analogy. The trial begins and the officer makes a definitive statement as to the speed you were traveling. You kindly ask the officer if she knows for certain you were speeding or was it a guess? She informs the court that she used a Light Detection and Ranging device, or LIDAR, to determine your speed. You continue your line of questioning about the device and ask if anyone has recently calibrated it, and the officer says yes. You view the LIDAR calibration report, and it indicates fluctuations in the results in nearly every test over thousands of tests.

Is there a court in this country that would trust the reliability of the detection device? That answer is easy. Of course not, nor should we accept its findings. The RCD problem is even more severe. At least with the LIDAR, we have known quantities, but with RCD, no one was there. We have documented fluctuations every few years over the last century, let alone tens of thousands of years, and we know the starting point compared to educated guesses.

Old-Earth proponents who rely heavily on RCD methods are not ignorant of these tremendous hurdles. In an attempt to overcome the debilitating problems, scientists began looking at other dating methods to assist with 14C dating. For example, they have cut down trees in a variety of locations around the globe and counted the tree rings.[31] They spent time at the bottom of various dried-up lakes collecting outcrop samples or drilled core samples from lakes so they could count the number of layers of silt, clay, leaves, etcetera, called lake varves, as well as drilling ice cores in a variety of glaciers to count ice rings.[32] The purpose of said scientific inquiries is to establish age via sources outside 14C RCD to compensate for the variances found in the carbon reservoir.

A second reason for spending time counting tree and ice rings and leaf layers around the world is due to what one scientist, Dr. Hans Suess, calls "wiggles."[33] Suess' discovery of large (hundreds of years) variations of age in the same product is a common occurrence in RCD. Scientists now call these universal anomalies "Suess wiggles and deviations."[34]

The next time you hear definitive dates, remember they aren't from a machine reading a product's date stamp. Like all computers, the results depend on the data entered by humans, which can be flawed. In essence, these dates come from tree ring counters, ice core analyzers, lake sediment sorters, and carbon isotope surveyors.

As a detective, a primary concern was the reliability of the aforementioned methods. If we were in court, in order to pronounce guilt or innocence, I would need hard evidence that is reliable. It turns out that none of the methods we count on are consistent.

First, we have already discussed the serious hurdles of carbon fluctuation. Second, trees do not produce a tree ring every year; sometimes, they produce multiple rings, and the fluctuations during the first few years of life are vast. This list is a short list of dendrochronology difficulties.

Professor William Doolittle from the Department of Geography and the Environment at the University of Texas at Austin lists many more concerns in one of his books simply titled *Dendrochronology*.[35]

Third, considering our surroundings in our brief lifetime exposes the serious problems that lake varve accuracy necessarily encounters. For example, storms, wind, and fire all affect the amount of leaves sinking to the bottom of a given lake. Some years will produce thick layers and some years, forest fires remove the leaves for that year and many years to come. When one takes into consideration the effects of drought over the centuries in countries where we have no record of events, how can one substantiate accurate lake varve measurements? Fourth, ice ring precision is fraught with difficulties.

I grew up in Pennsylvania, north of Pittsburgh. Needless to say, I know snow and lots of it. Anyone who has lived around snow for very long knows the incredible fluctuation in the amount one encounters from day to day and year to year. There are periods of time when specific areas receive large amounts of snow; the weather slightly warms and melts some of the layers, and a week later, another snow goes over the previous one.

This process repeats itself multiple times a year. I have shoveled snow where multiple ice rings were produced in a matter of weeks or less. In the colder climate of Greenland, these layers become covered year after year, crushing them down and making ice rings. The issue is that one ice ring does not necessarily indicate one year. Again, anyone who has lived in a snowy climate understands this innately.

Scientists are not ignorant of this fact and attempt to compensate by using a variety of methods, viz., (1) counting annual layers using both temperature and irradiation-dependent research (difficult if not impossible considering the data here is dependent on data elsewhere, or what is commonly called circular reasoning. It is illogical to support supposition A with supposition B when supposition B is supported by supposition A. A ladder cannot be holding a man if the man is holding the ladder.); (2) using pre-determined markers (think about how they got the markers; circular reasoning does not add credence to evidence. If anything, when those being questioned use circular rationalization, detectives take note because there is something they are not saying.); (3) radioactive dating of trapped gasses (consider this chapter on how those numbers come to exist); and (4) The Vostok Ice Core (widely considered the standard for ice-core dating; again, circular in nature).[36] Scientists document the serious flaws in ice ring core dating (see *Quaternary Dating Methods* chapter 5.5).[37] Yet, they seem to be okay with it when they also compare it to lake varves, tree rings, and carbon measurements.

The only unanswered question for a detective is motive. That is, why would brilliant, highly educated individuals seemingly ignore or work around the numerous inconsistencies associated with their research. Has their worldview tainted their perception of reality so much that they have difficulty accepting a lethally flawed hypothesis, or is there another veiled motive? I will leave this decision up to the reader.

RATE TEAM

From 1997 until 2005, a team of seven scientists with earned doctorates in their respective fields researched various theories in radiometric dating methods.[38] The team's degrees are in geology, theoretical physics, geophysics, and atmospheric science. The areas this team studied are radio haloes of Plutonium-218 decay, 14C, and nuclear decay rates. Their goal was to procedurally blank the mass spectrometer by identifying materials that at one time contained 14C but should no longer contain 14C due to its decay to the daughter element $t^{1/2}$14N. That is, the product is assumed to be older than 100,000 years, and all 14C has returned to its natural state of 14N.

The primary element the RATE team studied for RCD investigation was diamonds. They collected diamonds from twelve locations around the world. According to geological estimations, diamonds formed roughly ninety miles below the earth's surface hundreds of billions of years ago, much longer than the maximum 100,000 years to decay all 14C. The diamonds traveled to the surface when volcanic activity cracked the earth's surface, and magma rushed to the top, carrying the deeply buried diamonds. Miners often locate diamonds in the cracks called Lamporite and Kimberlite pipes.[39] Diamonds made from pure carbon hundreds of millions or one billion years ago should not contain any 14C. The RATE team chose diamonds due to the low probability of cross-contamination of 14C into the diamond sample. Soft body elements (e.g., bones) can more readily accept corruption from other radioactive elements in close proximity to the testable specimen. Conversely, hard elements such as diamonds do not have this drawback, as 14C should not penetrate the tough diamond (Items such as diamonds and bones do not absorb noticeable amounts of C14; living organisms ingest and deposit the same in their bones.). To further ensure clean samples, the team collected the test elements using the latest techniques used by scientists around the globe known to reduce and/or eliminate the possibility of cross-contamination.[40]

According to the belief that 14C decay rates do not fluctuate and the principle that diamonds are hundreds of millions of years old, there should be no trace of 14C remaining in diamonds. The RATE team found that each of the twelve diamonds had specific amounts of 14C.[41] That is, every inorganic sample contained low levels of 14C. The evidence is the same for both the OE and YE creationists. The only difference is the conclusion. A common retort by OE is the team used faulty methods; their samples were already contaminated at collection, machine background, and various other ideas to account for this discrepancy. If cross-contamination is possible for diamonds, then other softer element corruption will be even more severe, which calls the whole process into question.

The RATE team also dated ten samples of coal with the same results. Coal is a compressed organic material and is considered hundreds of millions of years old. Because coal is organic, it would contain 14C at burial. According to empirical and observable data, coal should not contain any 14C due to time elapse. Each of the specimens contains 14C.[42]

For both the diamonds and coal, either the empirical, observable, and repeatable science is false, or our preconceived notions are faulty. Perhaps the belief that everything is profoundly old is flawed.

CONCLUSION

While there appears to be some level of dependability in radiometric dating methods, there are also many questions that do not seem to have reliable answers at this time. At a minimum, the incontrovertible evidence of 14C remnants in the hardest naturally occurring element should cause one to pause and consider whether presuppositions or evidence are dictating one's conclusions.

If well-established scientific laws (e.g., causality, inertia, the effects of time on products like proteins) and a straightforward reading of Scripture suggest a young Earth, it's wise to reconsider the evidence. Ultimately, setting aside personal desires is essential for an honest evaluation of the available proofs. It is the weight of evidence that should dictate the direction within the scientific community, not one's hopes or desires. That is, after all, the core of the scientific method. Time and time again, science has caught up with the Bible. Man often believes one way, while the Bible teaches another. Truth, however, does not alter due to a whim or collaborative agreement; it is unchanging.

CHAPTER 7
COSMOLOGY

MAN OFTEN LOOKS into the heavens with wonderment as he considers the stars and his place among them, pondering, *What are they made of? Why do they stay where they are? How far are they? What's in between them?* And a variety of other intellectual and philosophical pursuits of truth and reality beg for answers.

Few matters make humankind feel more insignificant than when we consider outer space. The incomprehensible depth, breadth, and overall vastness are physically intimidating and intellectually numbing. Mankind has spent thousands of years trying to fathom our place in space, yet we have only begun to scratch the proverbial surface of understanding. Space is indeed the final frontier and something to marvel at.

Over the last few decades, humankind has spent billions of dollars sending exploratory rockets, some with animals and others with humans, in an attempt to gain a better grasp of our intriguing surroundings. This drive to know more about our universe has cost us more than money but also the lives of brave explorers. The benefits to the human race from this pursuit are vast. To most astrophysicists, it is not what we know; it is what we do not know that is most captivating. What astronomers are uncovering is the reality that our surroundings contain inconceivable mass and incalculable energy, all of which, although unseen, nevertheless exist.

Christians are often accused, sadly, rightly so, of not thinking critically about our surroundings despite the supposed contradictory scientific evidence. This chapter demonstrates to readers that the most advanced science is catching up to the Bible and verifying its integrity, not detracting from or disproving its contents. One can believe and study quantum physics, quantum mechanics, String Theory, and the Theory of Everything (T.O.E.) and remain intellectually honest while holding to Christian theological underpinnings.

DARK ENERGY AND DARK MASS

Please keep in mind as you read this chapter that this topic is deep and, at times, very difficult to grasp. Do not be concerned if you do not understand it completely; you are in good company. A renowned Nobel Prize winner in quantum mechanics quipped, "If you are not completely confused by quantum mechanics, you do not understand it."[1] The key to grappling with truth is not understanding something to its deepest level; after all, nothing we "know" reaches this level of inspection. The key is logically deducing and thinking critically through the available information, asking the appropriate questions, and accepting the conclusion of the evidence available to all who wish to research.

The newly discovered presence of unobservable items called dark energy and dark mass are altering our known laws of physics and making us reconsider their principles. According to scientific calculations, we can readily observe only 4.6% of all the energy and mass in the universe. The remaining forces are broken down to 23% cold dark matter (DM) and 73% dark energy (DE).[2] We cannot see these massive objects, yet we know they exist largely due to their gravitational pull on light.[3]

Our belief and current understanding of these two dominating factors of DM and DE began with Einstein's theory of relativity. In addition to Einstein's effect on man's grasp of gravity, he also influenced theorists to consider the possibility of increasing energy. He theorized space has the potential to continue to come into existence and thereby expand further, adding energy to the current total in the process.[4] As creation of more particles proceeds, they also bring with them large amounts of energy.

As previously mentioned, in 1992, the COBE (Cosmic Background Explorer) Space Satellite put one of the final pieces of evidence that scientists required to confirm the universe is continuing to expand and not collapsing on itself as gravity mandates.[5] The understanding of gravity prior to the confirmation of COBE required gravity to, in a sense, win, meaning the universe eventually will return to its original state of a small and incredibly dense ball, thereby crushing all that we know. In other words, we considered gravity the stronger force than the energy pushing things apart. This is a logical hypothesis if natural processes are the cause of the Big Bang. That is, we have a limited supply of energy, while gravity will continue to pull and push regardless of time because mass and gravity coexist. Prior to COBE's confirmation, there were some scientists who theorized a beginning to the universe, but until that moment, the debate raged.

A few years later, in 1998, the Hubble Space Telescope further confirmed the universe is still inflating, but not only expanding, it is picking up speed and not slowing, as science would predict, due to the power of gravity.[6] With this piece of evidence in hand, scientists reconsidered what Einstein hypothesized many years prior: the universe continues to expand while simultaneously creating energy, the cosmological constant.[7]

Scientists cannot directly observe said energy or mass, as it, similar to a black hole, does not reflect light. They have several points of evidence that indicate these objects exist, but they are transparent and thus only known to a select group of detection systems. As well as what we observe via bending or lensing of distant light.[8] The reason they title these masses and forces dark is that they do not know what they are; they are a paradox.[9] They are dark or unknown areas in science that not only may exist, but they must also exist in large quantities, as previously described. That is, roughly 95% (rounded up from 94.6%) of our universe we breathe in with every breath is untestable, unobservable, yet, overall, exerting massive amounts of force on our being, planet, and universe. While singularly, their impact is nearly inconsequential, corporately, we are forced to create an innovative scientific field of study as their combined effects alter our current grasp of reality.

We know DM exists for at least four reasons in addition to the aforementioned fact of galaxy push at increasing rates. First, stars within galaxies, including the Milky Way, are not responding as one would predict, given the observable surrounding masses. Gravity both pushes and pulls, and the wobble of many stars is not congruent with their surroundings. Second, clusters of galaxies exist in the universe. The mass and energy of these clusters have tremendous gravitational effects due to their overall or combined mass and energy, as opposed to what is typical of individual galaxies separated by great distances. Instead of these closely floating galaxies acting upon the well-established push and pull of gravity, they seem to somehow follow their own laws and move apart. Third, the temperatures of intracluster gases are too high to attribute entirely to the surrounding galaxies. This point is highly technical and beyond the scope of this book, but suffice to say, there is not enough observable energy to create the heat in the atoms surrounding the galaxies; it should be colder given space is near absolute zero. Fourth, as we observe distant stars, many of these light waves bend at predictable and expected degrees. Scientists refer to this phenomenon as gravitational lensing. Some distant starlight, however, bends at far greater degrees than the surrounding mass should allow. Something unseen is pulling or pushing the light waves to a greater level than the observable mass contained in galaxies. This unexpected and extraordinary gravitational lensing is cause to further substantiate DM.[10] There are other possibilities, but the study of DM and DE by theoretical physicists seems to answer more questions than others.

Even more pervasive than DM (23% of the universe) is DE (73% of the universe). Scientists determine the existence of DE in various ways, but the primary evidence is in the fact of a universe that continues to increase in size and expansion rates.[11] Scientists estimate the overall mass of the entire universe at 6e-51 or 0.000000000000000000000000000000000000000000000000006 kg (1.3e52 lb).[12] The amount of energy it takes to keep this inconceivable mass from crushing back on itself is beyond comprehension. Not only is it not compressing in on itself, but it is also inflating at ever-increasing rates. This is tantamount to a balloon continuing to inflate long after a person stops blowing into it but on an inconceivably large scale. Anyone witnessing a self-expanding balloon in the middle of a room would seek the answer to the *trick* because everyone knows balloons cannot cause expansion on their own. In the case of our enormous self-expanding universe, the question is: who or what is causing the *trick?* This fact alone mandates energy so powerful that it overrides all known laws of physics. Further, it is forcing the hands of quantum mechanics scientists and theoretical physicists to hypothesize from where said energy emanates. Enter String Theory and inflationary bubble multiverse, to name two.

A fascinating aspect of this notion is there are forces and masses beyond our ability to observe. They are clearly there and at work, altering the space-time continuum. The energies are so large and ever-expanding, a weight of untold volume swarming our very breath, and yet we cannot currently discern their existence, only their influence on what we can see. I believe these unseen forces and obstacles are, at a minimum, possibly man viewing the direct effects of God on His creation. Again, this is not an attempt to invoke the God of the gaps simply because we have a scientific black box. Instead, science's advancements are finally moving past the mundane of microorganisms that stupefied man into believing one's blood is wicked to what we have today: open black boxes exposing the reality of the invisible.[13]

The invisible and transparent apparitions of space are not hyperbole or speculation; they are there. We see their effect no different from wind; their existence is undeniable. The only difference is the conclusion one draws from the same evidence. Are the roughly 95% of the universe's hidden masses exerting force on everything that surrounds them to a greater extent than the enormous masses that are observable, and will these turn out to be something we simply could not detect with our current technology? Or is it possible that God is once again allowing mankind to scientifically and mathematically glimpse His existence, beyond what He has already revealed in the close-up nature of Earth? Either way, the Bible is clear, "The heavens declare the glory of God" (Psalm 19:1).

STRING THEORY

Einstein's Theory of Relativity works perfectly when applied to large objects or the macro-world. The micro-world or quantum sphere, however, does not play by the same rules. That is, gravity's effects appear nearly nonexistent at the quantum level, as well as multiple other scientific rules, theories, and laws that are unchangeable and well-known at the macro level. For instance, the smallest parts of atoms, such as quarks, can appear in two locations at one time or possibly travel faster than light (this is open for debate) and, at times, disappear and reappear somewhere different.[14] These tiny particles appear to, in a sense, vibrate similar to strings on an instrument, creating their movement and existence. As nature strums one chord, certain realities exist, but as the vibration changes, so do their appearance and/or presence. These observations led scientists to call their research String Theory (ST), as in the strings of a guitar.

Due directly to the fact that the macro and micro worlds are not supportable by the same theories, quantum physicist theorists began to hypothesize a variant view of this miniature world. From roughly the 1970s, speculations from these scientists have included ST.

The important aspect of ST for this project is the mathematical and theoretical possibility of additional dimensions. That is, over the last few decades, ST continues to indicate the possibility what we empirically know and understand may only be the beginning. Some ST scientists calculate at least ten (Superstring) additional dimensions beyond our three (four if one counts time) and up to as many as twenty-six (M-Theory) or more.[15]

The aspect of such real possibilities is further confirmation of God's word. God's word tells us that He exists but is currently invisible. The book of Colossians states, "He [Jesus Christ] is the image of the invisible God" (1:15a). Jesus made a statement recorded by Luke, alluding to the fact that everything spoken of by the prophets, intermittently exposed by God to man and currently hidden from view, is not distant, but instead close. Jesus stated, "You won't be able to say, 'Here it is!' or 'It is over there!' For the Kingdom of God is already among you" (17:21). This verse, at a minimum, makes it feasible for Heaven to be close and not far; that is, not a place we must travel to, but a place that is simply undetectable given our current faculties and nature. The straightforward interpretation of this verse is Jesus is God; therefore, wherever He is, so is Heaven, so Heaven was truly in their presence. This verse possibly intimates something greater; with our fallen sinful nature, we cannot grasp the dimensions (95%) of God's Kingdom that surround us. God is here, and it is feasible Heaven's dimensions are what scientists are detecting in quantum mechanics and cosmological advances.

It is indispensable for the reader to understand this author is in no manner implying God is limited by or contingent on the verification or falsification of stated laws of physics or any human concept. The allusion is that, for the first time in history, the scientific world is at the burgeoning stage of providing possible scientific answers (albeit unintentionally) to biblical concepts, which were at one point considered impossible.

The various pioneering theories are, in this writer's view, exposing the reality of what God said centuries ago, but man could not comprehend due to his inability to fathom the scientific depth of His words. The aforementioned innovations allow the Bible's record of second-order miracles (transcendent of natural and/or known scientific laws) to theoretically be recalculated as first-order (within the realm of natural and/or known scientific laws), while God remains transcendent of the same.

Miracles, by definition, are beyond scientific explanation, but the innovative world of theoretical science, at a minimum, opens them up to scientific empiricism as never before. This potential does not limit God or His miracles but, instead, offers a mysterious glimpse of His majesty and presence in His creation. The latest scientific theories do not explain away miracles, nor do they remove God; instead, they further substantiate the likelihood of the same. In other words, God, while He can and does maneuver outside said scientific principles, can perform at least some of the miracles without breaking one known theory of physics. God, who is Lord of all, has exclusive rights to disregard created laws, which He put in motion, and do as He pleases. It appears, however, to this theorist that God has rarely stepped outside of the laws He set in motion. Since the fall of man, we have had great difficulty properly perceiving God and His wholeness. As the end approaches, God may be opening up new avenues to know Him so that some may be saved from His wrath (Joel 2:28). These innovations do not hide or remove God; they further demonstrate His existence.

God had Paul write in the book of Romans, "For his invisible attributes, namely, his eternal power and divine nature, have been clearly perceived, ever since the creation of the world, in the things that have been made" (1:20). This writer suggests that God may be allowing additional exposure of His attributes than the relatively simplistic appreciation of yesterday, without altering the original meaning. Biblical texts have one meaning with multiple applications. That is, God has not changed anything; it is man's ability to rightly perceive that which has always been that is altering. This author likens these scientific revolutions to cell phones. All of the components, in particular the invisible waves on which the signal travels, have been in existence since God first created man. What would have appeared as a second-order miracle just a century ago (if not attributed to witchcraft or Satan) in the way of a cell phone for communication can today be assigned to a first-order miracle. Cell phones are an amazing and difficult scientific possibility to understand, yet true nonetheless and entirely acceptable by newly discovered scientific laws. Each of the components and laws needed to create such a device are first-order miracles. God may have given humankind many more venues that demonstrate His existence, power, and abilities as spoken of in the book of Romans than we even understand today, but we may tomorrow. The problem is not God but mankind. The sinful man had to open up to the seemingly impossible and realize such thoughts were only improbable. Science is catching up to the Bible, not the other way around, as promulgated for millennia by secularists.

Further, the Bible records events that do not contradict science's new grasp of reality but instead confirm the real possibility of the same. That is, according to quantum physics, particles can and do appear and disappear just as Jesus did after His resurrection (Luke 24:36; John 20:19). For millennia, the known laws of physics would not allow for such phenomena, but today the precepts are known and detectable.

The book of John recorded an event where Jesus walked through a door. Until very recently, science did not believe such an event was possible (I am not saying that science now believes humans can walk through objects, but if protons can do it, why, if we gained more understanding and control of the same, could we not? Again, what seemed impossible a year ago is now possible. Most importantly, Jesus was not corporal but was a glorified body.). Admittedly, John's recording of history does not explicitly state that Jesus appeared to walk through the door. What is interesting to this investigator is the fact that John mentioned the locked door at all. That is, it is possible the purpose of this comment was to signify the different appearance of Jesus in the room. The passage in the book of Luke referencing the same event does not talk about the door and employs the phrase, "Jesus himself stood among them" (24:36b) compared to John, who wrote, "The doors being locked ... Jesus came and stood among them" (20:19c-d). Luke gave the reader an understanding of the sudden appearance, whereas John painted a word picture of movement as supported by ST.

Quantum physics now recognizes the fact that particles do move through space, time, and matter with apparent ease.[16] Jesus, in His resurrected body, was following recently exposed laws of physics, which He created. Quantum tunneling (John 20:19 c-d) and quantum physics, in general, is where particles (i.e., mass) suddenly appear and disappear (Luke 24:36b). The glorified body of Christ was no longer bound by the limitations of the physical being of man, who was cursed by God in the Garden (Genesis 3:14-19).

This author contends that the moment Adam and Eve ate the forbidden fruit, the cut-off was immediate from the perfection in which they resided. Part of their fear likely came from their inability to see the dimensions of Heaven that we will one day witness again with our glorified bodies. Imagine losing the ability to observe 95% of what we know from previous experience surrounds us. The fear of such a change would be overwhelming. The Bible is clear that, once again, as Adam and Eve lived, so shall we, free from the confines of our frustrating three dimensions and into the limitless realm of God. It is impossible to fully grasp God's presence due to our current physical and cognitive limitations, but God makes it crystalline that it does surround our very being (Romans 1:20). It is a matter of passing from this limited shell to our true home with God via the blood of Christ (Romans 2:8-9).

To clarify, in no way is this project stating man's current understanding of physics or any other scientific theories and/or laws bind the God of the Bible. Clearly, the Creator of the universe transcends that which He created. The purpose of this section is to become a theoretical theologian and demonstrate that the Bible records some events that do not require the transcendence of physics. God appears to stay within His perfect laws that govern our universe. He simply expounds our understanding with His words and actions. If scientists would take seriously that which the Bible records and use it to hypothesize new laws, perhaps mankind could advance even further than our current standing.

THE SINGULARITY

Despite millennia of scientific belief that the universe is eternal, we now know that said understanding was erroneous. Scientists around the world now accept that the universe had a start. Astronomer Sir Fredrick Hoyle sarcastically called the beginning of the universe the Big Bang during a radio interview, and the name stuck.[17] Hoyle was referring to Lemaitre's 1927 proposal of the universe starting in a large explosion from a primeval atom.[18] Big Bang (BB) was a pejorative, not a compliment.

Upon establishing this remarkable watershed moment in astronomy and science as a whole, the Hubble Space Telescope unveiled an even greater mystery; the universe is continuing to expand despite everything we know about gravity, mass, and energy.[19] From those two powerful moments in the 1990s came the necessity for scientists to create new theories of how the universe came to be what it is today. This project has touched on String Theory, M-Theory, and T.O.E. (Theory of Everything) as scientific theories of defining where we have been, our current status, and where we may be heading.

Despite the innovative theories, the undesirable fact of a beginning is not going away. Scientists call this beginning of everything event a singularity. A singularity is where the laws of physics no longer work or apply, where space, time, and matter were in an "infinitesimally small" space, which then exploded and expanded, and after 14.5 billion years, we have what we observe today.[20] The question for this section is, if all aspects of the BB are accepted as naturalists embrace, how did what we detect in our solar system come to exist in its current state? More succinctly, how did planets form and begin to spin?

Astrophysicists inform us the planets came into existence by a multistep process of accretion. In its most rudimentary form, the accretion of planets occurs when small particles collide and coalesce around a small object in space and, through a variety of means, including electrostatic charge, slowly combine to create planetesimals. In time, these miniature planets collide with other planetesimals and eventually create a planet and/or star.[21]

While this is an interesting theory, like most theories, unless or until someone evaluates the mathematical, mechanical engineering, and physical possibilities, anyone can say anything they desire. Planet accretion has many hurdles to overcome in order for such a process to work to the depth that is required to both form a planet and then create spin.

A major barrier is the law of angular momentum. As particles, large and small, travel through space at great speeds, there is a specific and substantial amount of energy within this moving body. Similar in nature to Newton's Law of Conservation of Energy, a force of greater or equal magnitude is what slows or stops said object. In the vast majority of space collisions, one of the two colliding particles is at such a significant angle that upon impact, they simply bounce off of each other and continue on their way. The small amount of gravity from these miniature particles is not enough to overcome the value of the momentum within the elements and/or the pull or push from surrounding objects via gravity. Astrophysicist Erik Asphaug wrote, "It turns out to be surprisingly difficult for planetesimals to accrete mass during even the gentle collisions." [22] Asphaug speaks in this article about two primary forces that must be overcome for the disks to have any chance of forming: (1) Gravity's push and pull of larger masses near (relatively speaking) the small colliding particles and (2) The known energy of angular momentum.

Because astrophysicists are aware of this difficulty, they respond to the critics by stating that the formation of small jets occurs upon particle collision. [23] The jets of energy remove the energy from the particles, allowing the nearby larger particle's gravity to slow them down enough to enter a miniature orbit. [24] The elements that slow down are the ones that form the accretion disk that eventually become the planetesimals, which become the planet, moon, or star. To clarify, the answer astrophysicists offer for planet development is accretion disk formation. Several established, observable, and repeatable laws of physics work against the formation of these theoretical discs. [25] The reader must consider that we do not observe the aforementioned in space. We see dust, planets, and various particles that are said to be in various stages of accretion, but we don't observe jets of energy or collisions resulting in merging. The common retort is the process is so slow that we cannot watch it. First, the particles creating the dust we observe are already in close proximity. Second, said items are colliding but not combining. Third, space is expansive, and we can view millions of years in the past, so why do we not have several solid examples of this hypothesis? That is, while it may take large amounts of time, we can choose various increments of time depending on how far away we look. This means that we can slice billions of years of time into small segments, take our pick as to *when* we want to see, and witness that which we proffer. We do this, yet do not find what was hypothesized. Instead, we observe planets, stars, and spiral galaxies numbering in the trillions.

While there are disks of dust and various particles surrounding smaller and larger objects, there is little evidence that these disks are birthing new planets. It is more conceivable that an explosion, not accretion, is the cause of such collections that we observe around planets. Newton's Laws, the Law of Angular Momentum, gravity, and the mass loss associated with such slowdowns are physical barriers a scientist must overcome to imagine the low possibility of accretion disk formation. Even if, however, said events occur, scientists agree they would be extremely rare, yet we cannot count the number of stars and planets in the universe. Beyond all of these difficulties arises an even greater problem: where did the energy come from to cause the planet to spin after it formed? What physical mechanism made planets within the same solar system spin in opposite directions (retrograde rotation) from other planets while their moons spin and orbit planets in opposing directions, some around the same planet? I am not talking about "captured asteroids" we commonly call moons, but actual moons. Moons that are "captured asteroids" do not solve the issues just raised; they advance more questions than they answer, e.g., how did they form? Where did they come from (please do not say the magical, mysterious, and conveniently unobservable Ort Cloud while simultaneously mocking those who believe in an unobservable Creator)? Why did they stop where they stopped and begin to orbit? Why did they stop at that planet? Et cetera.

STAR BIRTH

In the previous section, one observes multiple scientific hindrances with planet formation theory. Despite the known, testable, and repeatable laws of physics that illuminate several serious obstacles to natural planet formation, some scientists use the same questionable methods to then explain star formation.[26]

It seems one unstable assumption leads to another unsound assumption. Anyone can make a statement based on a belief; it is an entirely different element when one must provide the mechanisms that make said statement possible.

For star formation, literature records that a diffuse cloud forms via an old star explosion (the circle of star life) or, as previously discussed, from accretion. The clouds of dust pull together via gravity to create a dense cloud of particles that eventually form the accretion disk. As gravity attracts the disk even tighter, it eventually forms a stellar system (star). Said star goes through multiple stages of life until it reaches a supernova, explodes, and dies. Some of this debris becomes another diffuse cloud, and the cycle begins again.[27]

Scientists point to the Eagle Nebula as evidence that stars are forming. In particular, an area of large dense clouds they call "Pillars of Creation."[28] This area appears surrounded by stars that astrophysicists tell us birthed from this region. They also point to the Orion nebula or M-17 as locations of continual star formation.[29] There is one problem: despite being able to see millions of years in the past, we do not directly observe any stars forming.[30] We do see clouds, which are hypothesized to be the parents of stars, but no direct evidence of said diffuse or accretion disk formations becoming stars.

Due to several factors, including distance, it is difficult to discern if the clouds are even near the stars, in front of them, or behind them. For example, when driving in the western United States, I have often believed there was nothing but a road between me and the mountains in the distance. As I traveled closer, I realized there were several other smaller mountains and many valleys in between.

In other words, due to size, distance, and perception, what I thought was accurate was actually wrong. As we peer into deep space, it is logical that our grasp of reality fades, similar to a road trip in the West. We have great difficulty understanding our own solar system, let alone other galaxies, and certainly not our universe.

Recently, astronomers announced they were wrong about Pluto being a planet—it is not. Additionally, Voyager 1 has entered an unexpected region, now referred to as the "space before space," a newly discovered area at the edge of our solar system. Tom Krimigis of the Voyager research team explained, "The new region isn't what we expected, but we've come to expect the unexpected from Voyager."[31]

There is nothing wrong with adjusting to newfound evidence; in fact, we must follow that logic. The problem, however, is such possibilities are ignored, and circumstantial evidence is put forward as fact with no explanation to the public of the possibility of complete error. That is, the star-birthing clouds are, at best, hopeful conjectures based on nothing more than preconceived beliefs that everything evolved from nothing.

In other words, as we look into space, we are technically looking back in time. If naturalistic evolution produced space, then there must be evidence supporting this claim. We should see at least some direct evidence (not circumstantial) other than a cloud of material, which could be many things other than a cloud that births stars. Some intellectually honest scientists admit to these glaring problems for star formation (i.e., no direct evidence of star formation anywhere in the universe) and respond with, "Given what we do observe, we can imagine (sic) what star formation looks like." [32] A scientist's imagination is required only because of presuppositions, not due to the known laws of physics.

If one's worldview emanates from Scripture, stars do not need to form but formed when God created them *in the beginning*. If the Bible is correct, we should scan the heavens looking for star deaths as things age and die, as the Bible describes (Genesis three). The fact is, star deaths are exactly what we observe by the dozens, and star births only occur in our imagination. So, who is following empirical science, and who is following a wish? Which of the aforementioned pieces of evidence would a judge strike from the evidence record as inadmissible because it is hearsay, and what proofs are readily observable and, therefore, admissible?

CONCLUSION

Astronomy is an intensely difficult and vast topic to study. Due, in part, to our limited grasp of the actual size of our Milky Way galaxy, let alone the universe as a whole, we attempt to understand what may be impossible on this side of Heaven. That fact, however, should not stop humankind from exploring with everything at our disposal the last frontier. God's creation is something to marvel at, ingest, and dissect (Genesis 1:28). This project submits that such exploration further exposes the beauty and grandeur of the Creator God of the Bible. Truth does not fear the inquiry of anyone, and God encourages us to seek Him (Matthew 6:33) and test Him (1 John 4:1). God does not confine such seeking to search of the Scriptures alone, but also investigating His handiwork at every possible turn. Quantum physics, quantum tunneling, String Theory, M-

Theory, Theory of Everything, and stellar formation are on the cutting edge of man's ability to grasp his surroundings, and investigation is deeply significant and exciting.

The unexpected result, at least by secularists, is the fact that such innovations do not alienate the Bible from science but instead expose the reliability of said ancient document as a trustworthy scientific document. To the believer, it is what we expect if the Bible is true. Our God is the Creator and Sustainer of all; therefore, He has firsthand knowledge of what scientists will find as they uncover and open scientific black boxes. Science is catching up to the Bible, not the other way around.

CHAPTER 8
EPIGENETICS

IN 1859, Charles Darwin proposed to the world the creation account recorded in the Bible is not how humans came into existence. Instead, Darwin postulated that all organisms, animal or plant, exist today via a process of natural selection, or survival of the fittest. Everything began with a simple single cell evolving into the complex organs and body structures we see today.[1]

At that time, and for many decades following, biologists had no reason to believe the cell was anything more than a blob of protoplasm.[2] It was easy for them to imagine one blob making another blob, as there was no understanding of the immense complexity that resides inside the protoplasmic dot.

BEYOND DARWIN

In 1990, a group of scientists began an audacious endeavor called the Genome Project, charged with mapping the roughly twenty- to twenty-five thousand individual gene sites and three billion chemical base pairs on the DNA molecule. The researchers completed said project thirteen years later, in April of 2003, with work currently continuing to fine-tune their findings.[3]

The scientific world and the community at large were rightly impressed with the intricate details provided by the Genome Project's conclusions. During this same period, a new and innovative scientific field emerged, focusing on a different aspect of DNA: epigenetics. Epigenetics, at its most basic level, is the study of heritable changes in individuals without an altered gene site, but the person is genetically affected.[4] That is, one's environment and life choices apparently change molecules that are on the rung of the gene site, and these alterations can pass onto one's child, but the gene site does not transform. That means that the consequences (i.e., physical and emotional) of a parent's life choices can be passed on to their children, and it appears to continually affect the epigenetic configuration for at least two generations and possibly more.[5]

CELL DISCOVERY

Humankind's burgeoning grasp of cellular life began in 1665 when Robert Hooke peered at cork through his microscope and observed small circular structures. Hooke used the term cell to describe what he saw, as it reminded him of a Monk's sleeping quarters in a monastery called cells.[6] Almost a decade later, another scientist, Anton Van Leeuwenhoek, first saw the living cell.[7] It took over one hundred sixty years (1838, or twenty-one years before Darwin published *The Origin of Species*) of cellular research for biologists to begin to grasp the importance of cells, or cell theory. Matthias Schleiden published the first cell theory book describing three main components: (1) the cell is the unit of structure, physiology, and organization in living things; (2) the cell retains a dual existence as a distinct entity and a building block in the construction of organisms; and (3) cells form by free-cell formation, similar to the formation of crystals (spontaneous generation).[8]

Science began its cellular expedition with the primal conceptions of Hooke and Schleiden and journeyed to the profound realization of today. Given our mechanical advances, and despite our efforts, we continue to only glance at the surface of the intricacy of the cell. We moved past the cell walls of Hooke, enhanced our view to reveal tiny organelles performing various cellular functions, looked even deeper to find the unimaginable beauty of DNA, and thought we were at the end of the depth of the cell, but we were wrong. There is yet another layer that has revealed itself to our technology, a code on top of a code. We call it the epigenetic code.[9]

DEOXYRIBONUCLEIC ACID: DNA

Deoxyribonucleic acid (DNA) is the building block of life. Without DNA, carbon life forms would not exist. The tightly wound strands contain and transfer their life-giving data from old cells to new cells via cellular mitosis.[10] Biologists estimate that cells die, and new ones replace them fifty to seventy billion times or more a day.[11]

The chemical makeup of DNA includes various elements such as hydrogen, oxygen, nitrogen, carbon, and phosphorus.[12] The area of direct interaction takes place in the rungs of the DNA ladder, correctly known as the gene sites on the double helix. Four primary elements create these connections: adenine (A), guanine (G), cytosine (C), and thymine (T). The A will almost always connect with the T, and the C will typically connect with the G (AGCT).[13] The AGCT connections are base pairs that are directly responsible for carrying one's physical composition during cellular reproduction.

Any error in base pairs, regardless of the cause (e.g., ultraviolet radiation, environmental, chemical ingestion, et cetera), usually leads to a mutation of the cell, and the majority of these are negative for the organism.[14] The damaged cell may recognize the error and self-destruct, or the host's white blood cells may attack it as a foreign invader and kill it, or it may lead to further mutations in subsequent cellular division, often leading to physical illness.

When a cell self-destructs or repairs itself, it uses what biologists call DNA repair systems.[15] Simply stated, cells have a machine that exists to recognize glitches within the cell and then somehow determines if the cell is beyond repair and self-destructs or fixes the problem and moves on. Please notice that this corrective mechanism works against the theory found at the core of Darwinian evolution; namely, parents transfer their genetic mutations to their offspring.

The DNA strand contains implausible amounts of data in a minuscule location, so much so that some scientists cannot believe it evolved. Some scientists believe the complexity of DNA is beyond Darwinian evolution's grasp and suggest DNA originated with aliens. They propose that intelligent life forms from a distant planet introduced the building block of life on this planet, with the intention of allowing it to evolve into what we observe today. Science refers to this hypothesis as panspermia or transpermia.[16] In other words, the information and artistic design found in DNA is so overwhelming as to lead ardent atheistic scientists to proclaim an extraterrestrial god or, in another sense, an intelligent designer.

DNA is so information-rich that just one gram could store the entire content of the internet. Warner Gitt, in *The Wonder of Man*, attempted to describe the vastness of the DNA strand. He penned that if DNA were a book, it would be equal to one hundred sets of thirty-volume encyclopedias. A top-tier typist, working eight hours per day, two hundred and twenty days per year, inputting three hundred words per minute every hour she worked, would take ninety-five years to type the data in one DNA strand. Or, if we could stretch out a pinhead (two millimeters (0.078 of an inch) in diameter) to the thinness of the DNA molecule, it would be thirty-three times longer than the Equator.[17] Physicist Lee Spetner wrote if we could flatten the DNA in all the cells in the human body and lay them end to end, they would easily stretch fifty billion kilometers.[*] That means light would take approximately two days to travel the entire length of the DNA in our body.[18]

Within each cell is roughly 1.8 meters of DNA. All totaled the quantity of our DNA would easily supersede the physical dimensions of a human body, let alone our tiny cells if specific functions were not in place. For instance, DNA twists and folds itself around a histone protein. This process reduces the territory, allows the strand to properly function, and keeps the cell from being overrun by the DNA alone. The chemical bonds of DNA and histone protein form to create the nucleosome.[19]

Recently, microbiologists discovered a DNA mystery. Biologists believed that if the DNA contained information, then said information would be useable as long as the specific gene site was "on." We now know this is not the full story. While the need to have DNA coding is necessary, it is how tightly the DNA wraps around the histone protein that determines if the DNA is useable or dormant, not just if the gene site is on or off. The critical nature of said discovery led to a new field of biological study, epigenetics.

EPIGENETICS

The word epigenetics has been around since 1942, when biologist C. H. Waddington coined the term.[20] What Waddington and science, in general, understood about genetics in 1942 did not begin to open the chromosomal black boxes we peer into today. His original intent of the word, a theory of how genes interact with their surroundings, is now fundamentally different as our understanding of the microbiological world has expanded. Today, scientists can view what one could only conjure up in one's imagination in 1942. Epigenetics of today, therefore, has a far more profound and intricate meaning backed by empirical rather than philosophical science. Epigeneticists try to understand how chemicals outside or on top of the DNA strand alter a cell's and, by extension, the body's physical, chemical, and psychological well-being.[21]

The word *epigenome* derives from the Greek word *epi*, meaning *on top*.[22] Hence, the word, simply put, is on top of the genome. The navigator, via various chemical processes such as methylation or gene expression, allows proteins to either travel down a given path or stop their progress and reroute their movement.[23] It is these quantum alterations that ultimately determine a genetic outcome.

Until 1996, biologists believed that biological alterations emanated primarily from DNA mutations within the gene sites.[24] Since the late 1990s, this field of study has continued to uncover that said belief is, to some degree, inaccurate. Yes, DNA mutations will alter a cell and sometimes the entire organism, but it is now apparent that alterations to the DNA are not required for physiological and, in some cases, psychological change. It is only necessary for a protein, a methyl protein, to attach itself to certain segments of the DNA.

When a methyl protein attaches to a DNA section, a process called methylation, the DNA wraps tighter around the histone, thereby shutting off its ability to replicate. Said section is methylated or unusable. The methylated strand cannot send signals to other proteins, thus making an entire section of one's

DNA completely inoperable.[25] While the cell can methylate a section, it also has the ability to remove the methyl protein, thereby making the once unusable segment of DNA operable. A key component is that these processes can occur repeatedly and never mutate or alter the gene site in any way.

EPIGENETICS AND OUR CHOICES AND ENVIRONMENT

Psychologists warn society about alcoholism, domestic abuse, and various other social maladies, as these negative traits transfer from one generation to the next. Biologists believe our deficiencies emanate from our chemical composition or nature.[26] Psychologists purport such disorders stem from one's environment or nurture.[27] The debate between nature versus nurture continues to rage.

Epigeneticists, however, pronounce a victor in this battle; it is both nature and nurture. [28] Arthuras Petronis wrote, "Thus, nature and nurture are not distinct and are certainly not at war."[29] How a caregiver raises her child has similar epigenetic alterations as the child's surrounding environment. Epigeneticists are altering the playing field of debate, and they are doing so with strong empirical data.

A study of dozens of families in Stockholm, Sweden, served as a catalyst to further research the ultimate effects of lifestyle on one's epigenome. In this study, sociologists and biologists collaborated on the effects of malnutrition caused by poor environmental conditions leading to drought, low crop yield, and eventually, malnourishment of an entire community.[30]

They discovered direct connections between the lifestyles of the subjects and their genetic displays. That is, good eating habits lengthened one's lifespan, while poor eating habits decreased it by an average of thirty-two years.[31] They also found the alteration transferred to one's sex genes.

This change is critical in that people's choices or mandates of today directly affect their tomorrow, their children, and possibly grandchildren.[32] Both the effects of one's physical environment and one's heritage directly affect the epigenome. One can rightly conclude that it does not matter if one's environment forces said lifestyle or if one chooses; the results are the same, as they both alter the epigenome. Nature, nurture, and personal selection change the present and future of the individual. Hence, one's actions or inactions affect him, his lineage, and, therefore, his community.

MAP, NAVIGATOR, AND CARTOGRAPHER

DNA is a detailed map containing details of each aspect of one's body. Nearly every part of a being is replaceable or repairable because of the protein map the DNA provides.[33] Due to a multiplicity of factors, there are, at times, errors or mutations in the map that can cause the cell to die, self-destruct, or, very rarely, produce other cells with identical mutations. As it turns out, that is as far as it goes; it is an information-packed map that requires a navigator: the epigenome.

Envision your GPS, which details a route to your chosen destination. The GPS knows of roads that will lead you there; all you have to do is follow them. What the GPS does not know is there is an accident on one of the streets completely blocking your route. Once you arrive at the stopped traffic, a police officer tells you the road is closed, and you must turn and use a different street. In a sense, you, the driver in this scenario, are the RNA responsible for the replication of the DNA. The road system, as known by the GPS, is our DNA. That is, it provides a possible but not always functioning route. The officer is the methyl protein closing off the typical route, forcing the RNA to skip the closed DNA road and move to the next area. The police can open the road if they clear the accident. This is no different than the DNA made available for replication if one's situation (physical and/or psychological) improves.

Similar to the study in Sweden, other investigations are discovering the direct impact of the environment on our genes. The key to these examinations is the fact that the environment is sometimes outside the control of the individual, or choice(s) can lead to an alteration of the personal environment. In other words, our environment (e.g., drought, famine, altitude, et cetera) regulates our genetic display, and if it is possible, we should remove ourselves from said harmful atmosphere. Additionally, it is one's personal inward development (e.g., thoughts, choices, stress, et cetera) that is of equal influence on the genome. So, regardless of my surroundings or my thoughts, both can lead to chemical modifications in the body, leading to epigenetic changes.[34]

As one lingers in a given scenario or continues to make poor choices and the epigenome changes, it becomes more difficult to switch back on and/or off than a simple one-time choice. Empirical science now reveals it is possible to alter one's gene expression despite one's nature and/or nurturing. That is, one can be born with predispositions and/or reared to respond in a given manner, but each has the authority to alter their genetic road map.

Hearsay is one thing, but the court of law mandates proof. Epigeneticists continue to unveil evidence unmasking the mystery behind free will and predetermination. Empiricism is tilting the scales held by the proverbial blindfolded lady of justice in favor of choice over genetic determination. Certainly, we may be born with a propensity to live one way or another; however, according to leading-edge science, it is our choice to change or remain purposely unmovable that holds us individually accountable.

While DNA is the map and the epigenome is the navigator, science is lacking the force behind it all, the cartographer. In other words, why does any of this happen at all, and where does the intricate detail exposing brilliance beyond comprehension start?

The tiny sites of the epigenome on a larger DNA molecule are listening to chemicals produced by various organs in the body. That is, ten to one hundred trillion cells, some separated by great distances (relatively speaking), work in unison to keep the organism alive.

If emergency circumstances arise, cellular-level altruism dominates to ensure the survival of the host. And minus the problems associated with illness and chemical interference, the human body functions with one goal: to live.

This book proposes that the cartographer if you will, is God. That is, similar to what the cartographer does, God is the motivating force who first gives life and secondly sustains its inconceivable daily functions as He directs and orchestrates the performance.

RESPONSIBILITY

In the movie *Spiderman*, Peter Parker's uncle, Ben, states, "With great power comes great responsibility."[35] While that line made for a good theatrical moment, Jesus said it first when He told His disciples, "Everyone to whom much was given, of him much will be required, and from him to whom they entrusted much, they will demand the more" (Luke 12:48). With epigenetic research, humankind knows our choices of today greatly influence our direction of tomorrow. While we have always been accountable to Jesus' words, modern science illuminates how this mandate is just and righteous beyond our simplistic grasp.

One can argue that the pinnacle of responsibility a human can embrace is the rearing of a child. Effective and attentive parents understand that their children closely monitor their decisions and often follow their example. Good parents, therefore, screen and alter their old ways to protect their children from their personal failures or sins. Before epigenetic studies, science understood one may be more predisposed than another to certain social or physical maladies if a parent(s) lived a life of moral failure. What we did not know is that even prior to conception, the choices of a parent(s) — good and bad — have a far-reaching effect on their child's predisposition. It appears the choices of a parent(s) predetermine a child's ability to properly function down to the genetic level. Further, this research indicates that said choices alter the gene sites for a few generations to come.

Randy Jirtle of Duke University wrote:

We've got to get people thinking more about what they do. They have a responsibility for their epigenome. Their genome they inherit, but their epigenome, they potentially can alter, particularly that of their children. *And that brings in responsibility, but it also brings in hope.* You're not necessarily stuck with this. *You can alter this.*[36] (Emphasis mine)

To clarify, a common defense for someone's illegal or immoral actions is that his deeds simply reflect his parents' training or cultural milieu. While epigenetics adds credence to this plea, it simultaneously takes it away. Because we are both nature and nurture, scientifically speaking, we must both admit outside influence while simultaneously and equally shouldering responsibility for our choices. Psychologically speaking, a person's choices of yesterday, as well as the final decision to go contrary to a cultural norm, are highly dependent on said personal decisions, in addition to their parent(s). Scientifically speaking, our thought life appears to have a direct effect on our cellular response to methylate, a given DNA segment, thereby altering our behavior.[37] And theologically speaking, we are accountable to God regardless.

"I lay the sins of the parents upon their children and grandchildren." (Exodus. 34:7)

Scripture is clear that each person is responsible for his or her own personal decisions to sin or not and will be rewarded or punished based on said choices (Deuteronomy. 24:16; Ezekiel. 18:20; et al.). Therefore, while man previously had no ability to fully grasp what this verse in the book of Exodus means, it is possible that it is speaking of the epigenetic alterations caused by the sinful choices of the parents. The writers of these words four thousand years ago could not possibly understand the ramifications of such choices at the scientific level that we can today. It is yet one more example of how the Bible has knowledge that only the Creator God could possibly know.

CONCLUSION

The research in epigenetics reveals that our physical, as well as spiritual health, is largely dependent on our parents' choices— and our personal choices. Nature and nurture appear to be in balance and not in opposition or an "either-or" choice. James Gills and Tom Woodward wrote, "... The genome and epigenome are linked to our health. Not only are aging and cancer linked to aspects of the epigenome, but many other diseases — including mental health problems — are likely to be tied to epigenetic changes."[38] They discuss how various researchers continue to correlate the epigenome with physical health. Each person's personal choices make alterations to the epigenome, thereby altering genetic expression. Health, it appears, is both nature and nurture, and one cannot continue to shift blame to parents alone but must take personal responsibility for one's actions or lack thereof.

Gills and Woodward delved into another aspect of the epigenome--the connection between the epigenome and spiritual health. Both authors agree that scientific research is uncovering facts that seem to buttress what Christians and Jews call *God's word* as found in the Bible. In particular, following God's directions ultimately leads one to a healthy life track physically, mentally, and spiritually.[39] That is, at a minimum, there is a correlation between what one reads in the Bible about death, sin, thought life, renewing of one's mind and body, and the epigenome.

While this book is not attempting to firmly substantiate a spiritual connection to the realm of the epigenome, it does offer a philosophical hypothesis that, at a minimum, makes specific claims found in Scripture scientifically feasible.

Science, therefore, appears to be moving in the direction of proving the validity of ideas from thousands of years ago and disclosing how said ideas are not only possible but also validated empirically. If this is true, and this author purports it to be so, philosophical scientists must inspect the Bible to understand its possible origin from a Creator who would know things that only a Creator could be knowledgeable about. For example, (1) imputation or transfer of sin from one generation to the next (Romans 5:15); (2) the sins of a father passing onto his offspring (Exodus 34:7); and (3) renewing of the mind affects the body (Romans 12:2).

For the first time in human history, man can read the systematic theological premise of sin imputation from a scientific basis. God's word states the result of Adam's sin is dying and that you shall die (Genesis 2:17). In addition to the reality of immediate spiritual death at the moment of Adam's first sin, there was also a genetic alteration. We can now grasp that the once-perfect DNA strand began to constrict around histones as methylation took place for the first time. The apparent limitless nature of man became limited both spiritually, via separation from God, and physically, through epigenome degradation (telomere deterioration and other DNA malfunctions also account for age limitations on humans regardless of improving medical science).

As one matures, the mind creates memories, and the retention of data affects one's DNA.[40] In particular, the modified DNA directly affects one's behavior.[41] I believe this innovative research reveals a greater depth of God's word than previously ascribed. That is, a passage such as the one found in the book of James 1:15 ("These desires give birth to sinful actions. And when sin is allowed to grow, it gives birth to death") illuminates the fact that the Creator God was speaking truth at multiple levels of understanding. It is difficult to miss James's intended meaning; i.e., a fantasy will likely become a reality unless put in check. The intriguing aspect of the verse is it may also be addressing a more intricate elucidation of a scientific fact discovered in the last ten years via epigenetics. At a minimum, this fascinating and innovative field of study does not negate the psychological or physiological parameters spoken by James. Instead, epigenetics demonstrates that as science unveils more mysterious areas of our DNA, God's word is not shown to be lacking in scientific information but, instead, is validated by ever-increasing technology and learning. The deeper we look and farther we travel, the more we realize this truth written long before humankind understood, and we find its genius in the sixty-six books we put together as one volume and call it the Bible. Once again, science is playing catch-up to the Bible, not the other way around.

The reach of this cutting-edge science is extensive if one follows the logical path on which it leads us. For example, teenagers often make statements indicating their poor choices to ingest drugs, overeat, eat poorly, become bulimic, or anorexic only affect them personally. What they fail to recognize are two authorities who contradict said statement: God in His word and scientists in epigenetic studies. A young person's thought life and physical selections, therefore, do not only affect the user; if they have children, they negatively impact their genome and likely that of their grandchildren.

Given the amount of collaborating research seeming to establish a connection between one's thought life and physical well-being, the following is a logical deduction. That is, if one controls his thought life by not allowing sinful thoughts and/or stress to dictate his day, his physical being will improve along with his spiritual being. While humanism (focus on self) claims similar results, the Bible commands one's concentration move from inward to outward or from self to God. Humanism holds a belief in self, while the Bible desires belief in an outside force — God — and it is the focus on God that produces a healthy well-being.

According to Scripture, we are born as people who desire to live contrary to God (Psalm 51:5). As we grow and mature, we have a choice to follow God or follow the ways of the world that are contrary to Him. If we choose to adhere to worldly ways, our habits become worldly (Romans 12:2). It is only through the renewing of one's mind via the power of the Holy Spirit that one can even hope to alter his path of self-destruction (Ephesians 4:24). One cannot renew his own mind as Humanism claims; it is only through the power of the Holy Spirit acting on an individual who has given his life to Jesus Christ through faith in His death and resurrection that one's mind can be renewed (Romans 10:9; Colossians 1:9, 3:10; et al.).

Imputation of sins and the sins of the father flow together at this juncture as epigenetics, at a minimum, makes such an intriguing possibility conceivable; one person's choices alter her genes, and those changes pass to the next generation and beyond (Exodus 34:7). The first sin of Adam permanently altered every human since that moment. We no longer prefer to honor God; we would rather honor self at the most fundamental yet physically critical levels, the epigenome. The sins of the father, therefore, do not simply nurture a boy to follow his dad's lead, but the poor choices of the father change the zygote, so the son's nature decays.

The longer humankind resides on this planet, the more genetic alterations will degrade. That is, one generation's depraved thoughts and actions build upon another, leading to a more volatile society with successive generations. The only hope for us is to turn to God and live as He has made us to live, as the Bible outlines. Minus such a drastic change, the end of humankind is inevitable. That is, we will become more corrupt as epigenetic influence builds upon negative epigenetic influence in a confluence of cultural evil where wrong will be considered right and right is considered wrong. We will believe our ways are true because, in a real sense, we are born that way. Our desires, recently considered evil, are now socially acceptable and said lifestyle must be our intended existence. Truth will necessarily become more difficult to decipher, as even the erudite and wise in the crowd will be under the hypnotic influence of the power of the deteriorating moral compass we call the epigenome. The incredible and encouraging aspect of this study is the knowledge that we are not confined to our epigenome influence; we can choose differently if we so desire. God, who knows the end, has already warned us of what is to come, and it appears we do not choose wisely.

In the last days, there will be very difficult times. People will love only themselves and their money. They will be boastful and proud, scoffing at God, disobedient to their parents, and ungrateful. They will consider nothing sacred. They will be unloving and unforgiving; they will slander others and have no self-control. They will be cruel and hate what is good. They will betray their friends, be reckless, be puffed up with pride, and love pleasure rather than God. They will act religiously, but they will reject the power that could make them godly. (2 Timothy 3:1-5 NLT)

Epigenetics does not contradict the Bible's claims, but further substantiates its validity. It is our own evil desires that destroy us (1 Peter 2:11). We would be prudent, therefore, to further our knowledge of the God who rescues us from our self-destructive thoughts, actions, and genetic malevolence.

"Then if my people who are called by my name will humble themselves and pray and seek my face and turn from their wicked ways, I will hear from heaven and will forgive their sins and restore their land." (2 Chronicles 7:14 NLT)

CHAPTER 9
THE HOW AND WHY OF APOLOGETICS

PEOPLE, in particular in the Western world, live hurried lives. Because of the tyranny of the urgent, we often fail to recognize what surrounds us and, thereby, are unable to analyze reality properly. We tend to simplify what our senses take in so that we can quickly move to the next issue, with little to no thought about what we are observing. To accomplish this task thousands of times a day, we use the default of evaluating truth based on our own varied background experiences.

Salvador Dali was a surrealist painter of the twentieth century. I observed his works firsthand at the Dali Museum in St. Petersburg, Florida. As I gazed at one of his paintings, *The Hallucinogenic Toreador*, an artist friend of mine, pointed out and explained various stories hidden within the large 13-foot x 9-foot painting. Dali purposely placed items in his paintings, small components that only the curious observer would find — stories within a story.

Near the bottom of *The Hallucinogenic Toreador* is an area that, at first glance, looks like nothing more than black-and-white dots. In time, and with the assistance of my friend, I saw there was much more than what first greets the eye. The white and black dots are actually a Dalmatian dog with its nose to the ground, tail in the air, walking toward a large maple tree during the fall of the year. Once my mind connected the dots, I came to understand there was a story hidden in what appeared to be nothing more than dots. Now that I have seen the dots for what they are, I will always vividly see a dog, leaves, and a tree.

The dog, leaves, and tree were always there; it just took effort and some help to see the truth that already was. Noticing the design created by the designer did not make me a smarter or better person, and I certainly cannot brag just because I recognized the truth. I did not change the picture, nor did I alter its design; I merely acknowledged its existence. Apologetics is a tool or friend that helps one see the design and, ultimately, the Designer. Christians are not smarter or better, nor can they brag about recognizing truth and the Truth Maker.

In a similar manner, the world and universe we live in are a work of art with recognizable beauty and miraculous complexity from macro to the micro. As one studies her surroundings, it does not take long before she recognizes the interrelatedness of this magnificent creation. The open mind concedes a grand designer must weave massive amounts of moving parts into one gigantic ensemble, like an oversized orchestra, where each one seems to complement the other as it works separately yet is not absent from the whole. It is the study of Christian apologetics that propels one from merely walking through life to a state of understanding that opens the mind's eye to the breathtaking reality of the existence of God.

For too long, academia has helped students memorize data but not interact with its application. Root learning, which has its use in limited areas of education, is largely an antiquated mechanism and of little use in apologetics. The reader should continually challenge his perception of data by listening critically to proffered information, gently processing for true intent, and judiciously interacting with it in order to truthfully engage and logically interpret truth claims with as little bias as possible. Media, Hollywood, friends, and coworkers will challenge a Christian's belief system via minuscule alterations of truth. The individual who uncritically absorbs information in a day of information overload is destined to fall prey to twisted truth. We must question everything in the name of intellectual, societal, and spiritual health.

APOLOGETICS DEFINED

Apologetics, from the Greek word *apologi,* means the act of supplying a verbal defense for one's belief system.[1] One can be an apologist for Pepsi, the Pittsburgh Steelers, widgets, and everything under the sun in which one holds strong beliefs.

The Bible, like a worthy head coach, does not take this subject lightly but instead commands that Jesus' followers prepare to defend the hope that is within them (Acts 22:1; 1 Corinthians 9:3; 2 Corinthians 10:5-6; Philippians 1:7; 1 Peter 3:15; et al.). A common response from fellow Christians is that apologists over-intellectualize and make it more difficult than what God intended. Christians in today's culture, therefore, must not only be ready to defend their faith with apologetics for the nonbelievers, but also for the believers.

Of first importance in Christian apologetics is the spiritual protection of the adherent in at least two ways. One, we easily convince ourselves that pursuing a specific course of action is rightful when, in fact, if its core were to be tested, it would be recognized as rotten. The Bible repeatedly warns the reader of the natural propensity to willingly follow sinful flesh rather than the righteousness of God (Genesis 3:6; 2 Samuel 3:4; Matthew 4:1, 5:28; James 1:14). We, therefore, must continually question our motives and actions to make certain that they are what God intends, and not necessarily what we want.

Second, life is a difficult and exhausting place where, eventually, everyone receives a dreadful blow to their psyche via various life events. In those moments, our feelings are likely to fail us. We will reach our psychological end. We find ourselves saying things such as, "I do not feel as if God loves me," or "I do not feel like talking to her about God," or "I do not sense I am saved." It is during those moments that one must rely on his cognition of spiritual data learned during the calm moments of the past and not depend on current events. In other words, when life is hard, and we cannot trust our emotions, we must trust what we know, or we will likely fail and rely on our rebellious nature for answers (Mark 4:19).

For example, in the book of Joshua, the Israelites were going through tough ordeals. The people began to question their dedication to YHWH (Yahweh). While in the difficult moment, their feelings failed them and their doubts about God's power and authority took over. Their desires became one of turning from YHWH toward the worship of the fake gods and idols of their past. The emotional state of the Israelites failed them, so they went to what they knew, false idols, and enslavement to same.

In chapter twenty-four, Joshua executed a brilliant apologetic to the people in an attempt to bring them back from self-destruction. He reminded them of what God had accomplished in the past. Failing feelings during a current tough situation does not alter the facts of yesterday. That is, circumstances and emotions change on a moment-by-moment basis, but God's presence and work remain. We, like Joshua, need to address the intellect so that we can know or recall *truth* and thereby override a desire to flee when things get tough and various feelings overwhelm our senses. The Bible calls humankind's need to intellectually grasp God's truth as a renewing of our mind (Romans 12:2; Ephesians 4:24; Colossians 3:10).

Third, the world proclaims that Christians, similar to Buddhists, Hindus, Muslims, et cetera., merely follow the ways of their culture and not reality. Apologetics, however, illuminates philosophical, scientific, historical, and theological certainty. It is, therefore, from a solid footing in substantiated truth that a Christian can stand tall, knowing beyond a shadow of a doubt that Jesus Christ is real and, by extension, His edicts are true.

Fourth, humans are inquisitive yet rightfully skeptical of grand claims. Those who do not question presentations of truth will certainly fall prey to lies (intentional or not). God repeatedly warned man to test what someone is peddling and not to follow every whim of man (1 Kings 13:18; Jeremiah 14:14; Matthew 7:15; 1 John 4:1). Hence, it is natural to question the veracity of anyone who claimed to be God, was crucified for said assertion, and rose from the dead. As one passively observes life, he intuitively understands such a notion is impossible, the ending in particular. It is amazing how quickly a Christian forgets how absurd such a claim as a resurrection from the dead sounds. It is insensitive and anti-intellectual not to be able to provide a reasoned response to a logical and rightful question such as: "How can someone rise from the dead?" A reasonable and thoughtful response to the most basic of questions is the minimum standard for Christian apologetics.

OFFENSIVE VS. DEFENSIVE

There are two types of Christian apologetics: offensive and defensive.[2] Offensive apologetics provides a rationale for belief in Christianity. The mandate for the same is found in the book of Second Corinthians: "We destroy arguments and every lofty opinion raised against the knowledge of God, and take every thought captive to obey Christ" (10:5). This passage instructs the reader to actively seek to discuss Christianity with those who do not have the knowledge.

Defensive apologetics occurs when a non-believer confronts a Christian with arguments against the precepts of God, Jesus Christ, the Bible, and other Christian beliefs. The decree to perform defensive apologetics is in the book of Philippians, "... You are all partakers with me of grace, both in my imprisonment and in the defense and confirmation of the gospel" (1:7c). The verse asks followers of Christ to be ready for the outright attacks from the world about the truth Christians proclaim.

Both are equally important and mandate preparation for the moment. There are, after all, many reasons people give for not believing in or following the call of Christ. Some will outright admit that they enjoy their lifestyle and do not wish to alter it for the sake of Christianity. Others speak about intellectual barriers, have no understanding of sin, do not grasp salvation, ardently proclaim the Bible is full of errors, and various other logical and/or illogical justifications. Christian apologists listen to what people question as truth so they can research the answer(s), accurately address legitimate doubts, and thereby defend the hope that is within them (1 Peter 3:15).

FOUR RULES

The act of apologetics is often contentious. There are three rules that the apologist should adhere to in order to reduce the possibility of a productive confrontation dissolving into a combative argument. First, the apologist should be in the process of building a relationship with the dissenter. That is, he needs to be real and humble (Ephesians 4:15). The association can be a momentary friendship and does not require months of meeting for coffee before a legitimate conversation about belief systems can begin. One can establish said rapport within a few minutes.

Second, an apologist must avoid becoming angry because of the other person's questions and/or assertions. A sincere kindness should rule the conversation (Revelation 20:10). Knowledge is power, and a properly prepared apologist possesses tremendous amounts of data. A questioner may feel as if the apologist is using a hammer instead of two loving arms to make his point. One cannot lose sight of the fact that the only reason a Christian grasps the truths of God is because of the enlightenment of the Holy Spirit, not her own intelligence. God created and is truth; no one has the right to brag for simply recognizing something that already exists. Christians cannot lose sight of the fact that what we believe and defend, the message of Jesus Christ, sounds irrational and foolish to the world (1 Corinthians 1:18).

Third, an apologist is required to care for the person with whom she is speaking (1 Corinthians 13:4). Having an honest debate is not about winning or losing; it is about spreading God's love found in the gospel of Jesus Christ. We do not succeed as Christians when we intellectually destroy our opponents and leave them demoralized and without hope. The intent of the confrontation must remain in the fore of the apologist's mind and thereby emulate a caring attitude for the individual, as opposed to a demoralizing victory.

A fourth key element in executing apologetics is active listening, dissecting verbal and non-verbal cues. To make this technique work, one must lace listening with critical thinking questions. People tend to tell you what they want to tell you and ignore those areas which contradict their beliefs. I have found that this omission is sometimes purposeful but more often unintentional.

That is, they were unaware of the shortfall of their view

until I listened carefully to what they said and followed up with a piercing question. I have found that asking someone to defend their view is the most effective in bringing about change, as compared to simply presenting copious amounts of supporting evidence. People do not like others telling them what to do or think, but when they convince themselves via self-questioning, change is easier. When you ask the right questions, their body language will tell you. Let the question sink in, and adding nothing at this moment is usually advisable. Allow them to think through the question and determine the legitimacy of the inquiry.

A few examples of good questions are simplistic yet profound: "What are your top two or three reasons you believe that?" "Define other ways to interpret the same evidence." "Describe your method of research." "What are the scientific mechanisms that make such action possible?"

I often say it is when we close our eyes to go to sleep that some questions linger and haunt our preconceived beliefs. The intellectually honest person will follow the truth rather than personal cravings. Truth is what we should seek and not ideology. Truth is the only rock that is not budged by the whims of man, the winds of time, or the echoes of the past.

DETECTIVE 101

As part of my police detective training, I took classes on interrogation techniques and handwriting analysis. Additionally, I have led or assisted in dozens of interrogations. The rule of thumb is that peoples' *truth* stories, verbal or written, are separated into thirds.

A person telling the truth naturally dissects and discusses events, with a third of their time spent talking about what transpired prior to the crime, one-third during and one-third after.

Generally speaking, any diversion from this pattern is unusual, and a detective will take note. Hence, in order to have a successful outcome, it is imperative that a detective concentrates on what the suspect does not say as opposed to what he does say.

For example, while I was interested in what the suspect did before and after the crime, it was his omission of detail for the two hours in which the crime occurred that grabbed my attention.

That is, why didn't he tell me about talking with the victim despite irrefutable evidence that said event occurred? Why did he spend a laborious thirty minutes discussing breakfast with his wife, only five minutes detailing the four hours after breakfast when the crime occurred, and another tiring forty-five minutes talking about his business lunch and afternoon? It was not what he said that mattered as much as what he did not say.

We focus on what we believe we know, mostly ignore what we do not know or doubt as true, and end with superfluous pontification to fill the void of ignorance. The wise apologist questions the middle third that is missing or left out of the conversation.

Jesus gave us several great examples of brilliant detective work and how to perform Christian apologetics properly. That is, He would often ask intrusive questions that penetrated to the heart of the individual's contention. His goal appears to have been one that allowed those opposing Him to realize their mistaken belief system more than Jesus pointing it out to them (defensive apologetics). For example, in the book of Mark, the Pharisees confronted Jesus, and the following conversation took place:

. . .

And they came again to Jerusalem. And as he was walking in the temple, the chief priests and the scribes and the elders came to him, and they said to him, "By what authority are you doing these things, or who gave you this authority to do them?" Jesus said to them, "I will ask you one question; answer me, and I will tell you by what authority I do these things. Was the baptism of John from heaven or from man? Answer me." And they discussed it with one another, saying, "If we say, 'From heaven,' he will say, 'Why then did you not believe him?' But shall we say, 'From man'?" — they were afraid of the people, for they all held that John really was a prophet. So they answered Jesus, "We do not know." And Jesus said to them, "Neither will I tell you by what authority I do these things." (11:27-33).

The spiritual leaders of His time attempted to trap Jesus with a line of questioning intended to snare Christ in a theological corner. Jesus saw past their challenge and put them on the spot. The last few verses allow a glimpse into what occurs in the minds of those who eventually realize they have nothing philosophical or theological to use as a defense. This is what critical thinking and suspicious questioning affords the astute apologist.

A fifth and most essential aspect of apologetics is the importance of complete dependence on the leading of the Holy Spirit. The Bible is clear; the follower of Christ can do nothing of lasting value outside the authority of the Holy Spirit (John 14:26). We must rely on His leading, direction, and recall before, during, and after the verbal apologetic debate. Minus this authority, our personal power of persuasion, regardless of how logically convincing, will fall on deaf ears (Matthew 22:37).

CHAPTER 10
SIX LITERAL DAYS

A FOX NEWS poll indicates that nearly half of all Americans believe in a created world, as outlined in the book of Genesis.[1] Polls are not what determine truth, but it is an interesting statistic when one considers that the entire public education system has adamantly pushed its agenda for decades, with little to no opposition permitted in the classroom.

Additionally, some science channels on television (e.g., NatGeo, Science, Discovery, et al.) continually promote evolution as factual and seem to promote that only the uneducated would believe otherwise. Statistics, as found in the Fox News poll and others, seem to indicate that mankind instinctively recognizes there is something inherently askew with the theory of evolution or Neo-Darwinism. Pro-evolutionists have become increasingly agitated with the public's refusal to accept their view of the evidence, so they beat their drum louder, attempting to drown out any opposition.

A CHRISTIAN DEBATE

A common debate among creationists is whether God created everything in six literal 24-hour days about 6,000 to 10,000 years ago, or over billions of years. In my opinion, it's essential to understand both perspectives and form a decision based on all available evidence, not on presuppositions, hopes, or desires. This topic should not be a source of division, but rather an opportunity for both sides to seek the truth together.

In this chapter, I use a historical-grammatical method of interpretation. This approach uses a scientific method found in biblical hermeneutics (the science and art of biblical interpretation). Employing said method takes into account the syntax, historical background, cultural aspects, and literary genre. It is important to recognize there are solid Christians who believe that a literal interpretation of the book of Genesis indicates large spans of time and evolution to some level used by God to create, while others understand the same evidence supports the notion that God created everything in six literal twenty-four hour days roughly 6-10,000 years ago. I am not asserting that one's belief in one or the other indicates salvation.

UNDERSTANDING THE VARIOUS VIEWS

While this chapter briefly explores two possible solutions (generally referred to as young and old creationists), it is important to note there are several other opinions held by some Christians. For example: (1) Flat-Earthers, (2) Geocentrists, (3) Evolutionary Creationists, (4) Theistic Evolutionists, (5) Methodological Materialistic Evolutionists, and (6) Philosophical Materialistic Evolutionists.[2]

Flat Earthers (In my opinion, those who are detached from reality) are a minority of individuals who continue to believe that the earth is flat. Their decision to follow this concept relies heavily on an exaggerated interpretation of the Bible from passages that describe the world as having four corners (Isaiah 11:12; Revelation 7:1), the earth has ends (Job 38:13; Jeremiah

16:19), and the earth is a circle and not a sphere (Isaiah 40:22). What they fail to recognize is that those metaphors are still used in normal speech today.

Geocentrists deny the validity of current science or heliocentric cosmology that states the earth moves around the sun. They believe that the Bible and scientific laws indicate the earth does not move, but the sun and planets revolve around the earth. Their primary biblical argument is found in the book of Psalm 93:1 "...the world also is established, that it cannot be moved" (KJV). They substantiate the definition of "moved" by looking at other passages that use the same Hebrew word to then assert that God's intention is for man to understand the earth does not move (1 Chronicles 16:30; Psalm 16:8, 96:10). One of the most prominent proponents of this movement is astrophysicist Gerardus Bouw Ph.D. Beyond Scripture, Bouw details scientific explanations to further support the geocentric point of view.[3]

Evolutionary Creationists (EC) and Theistic Evolutionists (TE) are similar in their cosmology but differ in their theology. ECs believe that it is God who created both the physical properties and evolutionary processes that led to what we observe today. Theologically speaking, ECs allow for a true Adam and Eve and the need for a Savior in Jesus Christ. That is, God began the process, but man destroyed His good intentions after his ontological leap to a soul. TEs, on the other hand, invoke God into science where the theories and laws appear to end and do not provide an adequate explanation; it is the classic "God of the gaps" explanation. Again, God was the impetus to all things, but unlike the ECs, where God steps back and allows evolution to be the deciding force, the TEs' God occasionally visits His creation.

Methodological Materialistic Evolutionists (MME) leave room for a god, but that god, at most, is responsible for the creation of the evolutionary processes, not the creation of all matter that controls all beings, present and future. For the most part, MMEs remain silent about God, are not atheistic per se, and generally consider themselves nonreligious.[4]

Philosophical Materialistic Evolutionists (PME) do not believe in a god of any kind. They are completely atheistic in nature and invoke natural processes alone. One of the most prominent supporters and staunch defenders of the PME position is Richard Dawkins.[5]

OLD-EARTH AND YOUNG-EARTH CREATIONISTS

Old-Earth Creationists (OEC) accept the various scientific theories that claim the earth, and all other cosmological items are billions of years old. They, like Young-Earth Creationists (YEC), unbendingly hold to a need for the God of the Bible as the Creator of the universe and all things seen and unseen. The primary divergences are their scientific rather than theological interpretations of the same scientific evidence. However, detailed theological interpretations vary at some critical points as well. Douglas Potter of Southern Evangelical Seminary, an Old-Earth proponent, believes there is more to this discussion and states:

"I think it is more than interpretation, that is the surface level of detecting the difference, the actual differences are methodological, one uses the Bible (or should I say their interpretation of it) as a filter for science [YEC], the other [OEC] uses a two-way dialogue between their interpretations of God's world and word that favors the more certain evidence given a conflict."[6]

OEC's are broken into four subcategories: (1) Gap Theory, (2) Day-Age, (3) Progressive, and (4) Intelligent Design. Each of these suppositions holds to the aforementioned premise of

the existence of the God of the Bible but differs in His involvement, time, and interpretation of specific Hebrew words
dealing with creation found in the Bible.

The Gap Theory (GP) or Ruin and Reconstruction Theory
(RRT) affirms a contextual interpretation of a long period of
time (i.e., a gap of time) in the book of Genesis, chapter one,
between verses one and two.[7] The secondary term of RRT
emanates from the interpretation of the book of Genesis, "The
earth was formless and void" (1:2a). They state His intention
was to signify a large period of time, filled with the creation of
life ending in death as the creatures adapted to their surroundings. How much time elapsed is open for debate, but most GPs
accept millions if not billions of years and massive amounts of
evolutionary processes.

The Day-Age Theory (DAT) maintains the God of the
Bible never intended for mankind to believe that His creation
period of time was similar to what we observe today, i.e.,
twenty-four-hour periods of time. Instead, each description of a
day signifies an unquantified period of time. Their primary tool
for said interpretation is defining the word day in these verses
or the Hebrew word *yom*. In the Bible, *yom* is, at times, an
unspecified period of time (Genesis 2:4). In some Bible verses,
the same word indicates a specific period of time (Genesis
7:11).[8]

The Progressive Theory (PT) is similar in philosophy to
TE theory in that they both see the hand of God revisiting His
creation to impose His will. The fundamental difference is TE
views God's hand as moving His creation in a certain direction,
but not creating anything new (macroevolution). PTs believe
God supplies macroevolution, while microevolution works on
its own, as God put biological laws in motion (adaptation).[9]

INTELLIGENT DESIGN

Intelligent Design (ID) advocates support the notion that intelligence begets intelligence and life does not come from non-life.[10] It is a form of teleological argumentation that contends complexity of life must emanate from other forms of complexity. It is from this premise that ID debates that a naturalistic BB does not create order but, instead, chaos.[11]

The ID movement employs a few key arguments: (1) Irreducible Complexity, (2) Specified Complexity, (3) Fine Tuned Universe, and (4) Intelligent Designer. Each of these topics directs the individual to the aforementioned case of what we observe cannot have simply occurred by random chance, as promulgated by EC, TE, or MME supporters.

Irreducible complexity speaks directly to the microbiological level recently uncovered via innovative technology. It demonstrates that products such as the flagellum motor that propels microbes could not have been formed over any extended period of time because if you take one part away, the whole thing becomes cumbersome and not a beneficial mutation.[12]

Specified complexity asserts that when something in biology is both specific and complex, and it combines forces to create a useable and/or necessary product aiding in the survival of a given creature, then that product must have come from an equally complex and specified force, not via evolutionary processes. William Dembski, who is widely considered the father of said theory as applied in the ID movement, wrote, "A single letter of the alphabet is specified without being complex. A long sentence of random letters is complex without being specified. A Shakespearean sonnet is both complex and specified."[13]

When ID uses the term "Fine-Tuned Universe," it is saying

that the earth's location, the laws of physics, gravitational force, weak force, strong force, chemical makeups, et cetera are so precise and constant that, if they were not as they are, life would not be possible. Said factors appear set by an intelligence greater than ours to such a measure that chance and time cannot account for such precision.[14]

Lastly, according to ID, an intelligent designer is the power or authority that supports and upholds the laws that created and continue to govern said irreducibly complex organisms, specified complex compounds, and a fine-tuned universe. Depending on the scientists within the ID movement, the so-called designer has various roles, from intimate involvement to the initiator of some things but no longer part of the process. The fact remains that ID strongly supports the necessity for a transcendent being or force that initiates the governing scientific laws, thus allowing life to exist.

The scientific community generally mocks and/or outright rejects appeals to greater intelligence, such as an intelligent designer. This same group, however, spends billions of dollars and untold man-hours searching the universe for intelligent life beyond ours that may have its own genesis story and may be responsible for beginning life on Earth.

SETI is one such example of scanning the universe for the "aliens" who were the impetus to life on Earth.[15] Additionally, the infamous militant atheist Richard Dawkins admitted to the possibility of aliens being the genesis of life on Earth.[16] The idea has such a footing in scientific thought that it has a title, panspermia, and this topic was given time for a lecture to fellow high-level scientists at a recent NASA conference.[17]

The point of this remark is to emphasize the fact that serious scientists are giving thoughtful consideration to aliens being the cause of the effect we see today. The question this lowly detective asks is, "If we find aliens, and what an exciting thought that is, will we not be back to the same question? That is, what was the cause that created the effect we just found?"

Maybe, if there are creatures out there, they are traveling down the same intellectual and philosophical physics road as we are, seeking their own cause. Because we see the laws of physics working the same across space, including mysterious quantum fluctuations, their epistemological search must, therefore, be similar in nature. They may be further down the road of *solving* string theory, but does that solve the issue of the cause of the vibrations or the strings?

Ultimately, no matter how deep we travel in space or time, humankind is left with the same question to an unbending, well-established, continually supported law we call "cause and effect."

Searching the universe for intelligence greater than ours is not abnormal; the only difference between the secularists and the religious is the anticipated result of said exploration. That is, the evidence is clear to both groups; life on earth shows implausible specified complexity that is inexplicable via neo-Darwinian processes.

All good scientists follow the scientific model that mandates that if the tests do not substantiate the hypothesis, the hypothesis must change, not the evidence. In other words, the evidence dictates the direction of the research, not the antithesis.

Decade after decade, test after test continues to reveal to a reluctant humankind that our existence is so unique that even the unimaginable is possible (Occam's Razor): a being of greater intelligence than ours exists, and said being may be an alien or it may be God. If it is an alien, we are back to square one. Where did the aliens come from? Physicist Dr. Michio Kaku rightly defended our known laws of science when he argued that we can logically defend the need for the existence of God because we do not know where we came from (He specifically talks about String Theory, Bubble Universe theory, et cetera, but the same physics principle of cause and effect applies.).

Young-Earth Creationists (YEC) also interpret the Bible literally, believing that it indicates God created everything in six literal twenty-four-hour periods of time roughly 6,000 years ago. YEC and OEC agree on nearly every theological issue in the sense that the God of the Bible is the Creator and sustainer of all. The primary difference between these two series of thoughts is the timing of said events. OEC view the biblical and scientific evidence as indicating a long span of time in the millions or billions of years, while the YEC view the same evidence as demonstrating creation was fairly recent (6-10,000 years ago). Both factions have good evidence to support their conclusions and warrant closer inspection.

PRESUPPOSITIONS AND WHY THE INVESTIGATION

Due to my a priori knowledge, I firmly believe the following presuppositions: (1) Man wrote the Bible inspired by the Creator God to record events and/or future occurrences so that mankind could know their God. (2) The Bible is inerrant in its original form, and the books we hold today that we call the Bible (excluding improperly interpreted versions) are very close to the original. (3) Various people, cultures, and religious groups have intentionally and unintentionally altered and maligned the Bible. God, however, has miraculously protected thousands of extant manuscripts from the second and third century that scholars and theologians use to ensure what we read today is accurate, despite thousands of years of inappropriate alterations, in particular during the so-called "Dark Ages." (4) Similar to other historical recordings, the Bible is to be taken literally unless or until the evidence indicates otherwise. A literal interpretation will often include allegories, metaphors, and similes. It is the reader's responsibility to employ proper interpretative means to know when the Bible changes from actual events and descriptions to something outside of a straightforward literal interpretation.

It is common for Christians to argue that studying how God started it all is nearly irrelevant, at best, and divisive, at worst. One's belief, however, on the topic of creation is important on several levels. An essential question most serious thinking humans ask is how we got here, and the study of creation attempts to answer said question. If man came about by natural processes as naturalists proclaim, then we will simply return to dirt and there is no need to delve any further. If, however, we are a creation of a higher power or a god, then it would seem rational to believe that he, she, or it will one day hold us accountable for what we did with our existence that he allowed.

The Bible makes it clear that God is the Creator of all, seen and unseen (book of Genesis). Billions of people groups and various religious assemblies believe said statement (Islam, Judaism, Christianity, Mormon, et al.).

With such a massive force of believers, it is, at a minimum, prudent to examine what and why they so strongly hold to such beliefs. This is not a philosophical/logical fallacy Argumentum ad Verecundiam or appeal to authority, but simply a note of logic.

That is, if millions of people from multiple cultures believe something, is it not rational, at least, to evaluate their claim(s)? It is no different from when someone tells me the majority of scientists believe in naturalistic evolution. Because that statistic is accurate, I have spent years of my life investigating their evolutionary claims. I find it intellectually judicious to put energy into claims of truth when wise and intelligent people

proffer a view, regardless of whether it differs from my preconceived notions. Truth matters.

Jesus Christ often referred to the creation events (Luke
11:50; Mark 10:6; et al.). As a follower of Jesus, it is theologically compulsory to investigate His teachings on said topic. If
Jesus was inaccurate in His references, this error must call into
question His validity as a Savior. Jesus could not, then, be
omnipotent and thus not a perfect sacrifice for sins.

OLD-EARTH AND YOUNG-EARTH CREATIONISTS DEBATE

Of primary importance in this debate is understanding that
both OEC and YEC view all data, including scientific, through
a biblical worldview lens. They believe the Bible is truth and
the only way to truly grasp all reality is to first know what the
Creator intends for humankind.

This system is no different from the way any individual
approaches evidence of any kind. Atheistic scientists' worldview lens is naturalism, and they seek answers from various
particles and their corresponding products, from rocks to
quasars. While the arguments are extensive on both sides,
OEC and YEC, this project lists only a few of the most prominent arguments that each side proffers as evidence, signaling
their belief system is the most trustworthy.

The greatest contention between the two camps is the
assertion by the YEC that the book of Genesis makes it clear
that *yom* and the surrounding verbiage indicate God's intention
of indicating His creation took six twenty-four hour periods of
time, while the OEC say it is unspecified time. OEC rightly
illuminate the fact that *yom* is often an unknown period of time
(e.g., Genesis 18:11, 24:1; Joshua 23:1; Zechariah 8:4; et al.).
YEC agree with the OEC on this point. YEC, however, make

an exception for when *yom* is contained in a context specifying the period of time, known as a declarative.

John McArthur wrote in his study Bible that Genesis chapter one, verses three through thirty-one, indicates God used six twenty-four-hour periods of time. He made this claim because "day," with numerical adjectives in Hebrew, always refers to a twenty-four-hour period.[18] He also wrote, "Scripture does not support a creation date earlier than 10,000 years ago."[19]

Gleason Archer disagreed with McArthur when he wrote:

In Hebrew prose of this genre, the definite article was generally used where the noun was intended to be definite; only in poetic style could it be omitted. The same is true with the rest of the six days; they all lack the definite article. Thus they are well adapted to a sequential pattern, rather than to strictly delimited units of time.[20]

Norman Geisler also disagreed with McArthur. Geisler admitted the declarative statements of the book of Genesis, chapter one are a possible interpretation, but such explanation is not required, as there is no such rule in Hebrew writing.[21] He also stated if one does decipher said passages as literal days, they do not necessarily equate to solar days as we understand them today.[22]

Barry Leventhal of Southern Evangelical Seminary, a Messianic Jew who speaks Hebrew, stated:

Genesis chapter one indicates each day is a literal twenty-four-hour period of time. Hebrew grammar mandates this understanding. Just because, however, this is true, that does not automatically indicate the earth is young. There are many options prior to said statements that allow for greater periods of time.[23]

The word *yom* occurs over two thousand times in the Old Testament, roughly forty-two times outside of the book of Genesis. We use the word "roughly" because the YEC contend that some of the passages the OEC count as applying to this argument do not, and YEC reduce the number to twenty-three.[24] The declarative words "evening" and "morning" with the word "yom" occur twelve times (Exodus 27:21; Leviticus 24:3; 1 Chronicles 16:40; 2 Chronicles 2:4, 13:11; Ezra 3:3; Job 4:20; Psalm 55:17, 65:8; Ezekiel 24:18; Daniel 8:14, 26).

Of the twelve, only one does not directly refer to a twenty-four-hour period of time (Psalm 65:8). Both factions use this as an example of why their belief is the most sensible. That is, OEC say Psalm 65:8 demonstrates that it is possible for yom, despite its use with a contextual declarative period of time, to indicate an unspecified period of time. YEC, on the other hand, say that Psalm 65:8 is one of many examples that lightly, yet not conclusively, demonstrates "yom" with contextual barriers can indicate unspecified periods of time.

A second contention by YEC is Jesus' statement, "Therefore, just as sin came into the world through one man, and death through sin" (Romans 5:12a). YEC contend this statement is imprecise and calls His deity into question. That is, if there were millions of years of evolution prior to Adam, then death was around long before Adam's creation and subsequent sin. Some OEC proponents state such a claim is preposterous because God is not concerned with the salvation of animals. God's focus is on the salvation of mankind. Hence, when Jesus made this statement, He was referring to the death of a human,

not an animal.[25] OEC contend that YEC take this literal statement further than it should and is forcing a non-existent issue.

Thirdly, YEC argue that OEC have set science ahead of
the Bible. They do this, YEC assert, when agreeing with the
conclusions of the majority of scientists who declare geologic
and astronomical indications demonstrate millions of years, not
thousands of years. YEC interpret the same scientific evidence
put forth by OEC as repeatedly exposing fallacious assumptions and unwarranted conclusions.

A fourth controversy revolves around the omnipotence of
God. That is, the question is not "How can God create all
things in six literal days," but instead, "Why did He take so
long?" YEC contend that God could have created all things and
more in a moment, but He purposely chose seven days as an
example for mankind (Exodus 23:12). His creation time was
purposeful, neither slow nor fast. He preplanned a specific
period of time, in part, to demonstrate to man how his work
week should take place; work six days and take a day off to rest
his body and mind (Exodus 34:21).

OEC generally do not disagree with the aforementioned
assertion; they dispute the juxtaposition. That is, both parties
agree God transcends all things, including time, and His
command is to rest on the seventh day. OEC do not agree with
YEC with the connection of Genesis one and Exodus thirty-
two or thirty-four. Confining God to six literal days because He
uses it as an example in another time and location does not
necessitate six twenty-four-hour days. Again, this argument
rests on one's interpretation of yom, and, thus, why that study
warrants greater depth than intended with this project.

CONCLUSION

The debate between OEC and YEC is captivating. It is this writer's contention that demonstrating God as the Creator is of principal importance. Internal Christian squabbles should occur behind closed doors so as not to disturb the progress of the gospel. The world has enough doubts. Seeing contention among God's people over a debatable topic is senseless and begs the question of whether some simply wish to demonstrate their supposed intellect over their humility to follow a God who mandates full and eternal submission to their Master.

This chapter is a cursory search of the relevant data. This topic warrants a full dissertation. At no point should such debate lead to brotherly division, but instead, a close bond should form as they struggle to comprehend the Almighty God.

CHAPTER 11
A FINAL THOUGHT

THE BOOK of Hebrews chapter one informs the reader that faith is the substance, or evidence, of things unseen. Faith is something that begins with facts, leading to a journey that moves past proof and into wondrous lands of unknown and intriguing reality. The study of apologetics is one of the best ways to reach said destination.

This book exists so that the reader may know who the Creator God is, His completed work on Calvary, and His love for each and every soul. This book is a failure if the reader misses this point. It exists to glorify and honor the risen Savior Jesus Christ.

Salvation is first being justified (Acts 13:39), or declared righteous in legal terminology, by one's faith (Acts 15:9) in the completed work of Jesus Christ. Upon putting faith in the blood of Christ, one spends her life becoming sanctified by the power of the Holy Spirit (Romans 7:24-25, 8:13; Colossians 3:5; et al.).

That is, accepting the free gift of salvation via one's faith begins a process of sanctification, which is a long race, not a sprint (1 Corinthians 9:24), and one must count the cost (Luke

14:28) of following a King who the world hates and would desire to kill again if He presented Himself as a mortal man. Following Christ (i.e., accepting His grace via one's faith) is a difficult path, which is becoming more perilous as the times grow increasingly evil. The difficulty rests in one's ability to withstand the onslaught of evil men who wish to, at *a minimum*, marginalize Christianity and, at worst, destroy its existence. One's salvation does not reside in individual abilities or inabilities; it rests in the hands of Jesus, and removal from Him is impossible (John 10:29).

It is not that following Christ as biblically prescribed equates to salvation or that Jesus must dominate (Lordship theology) one's life in order to be saved from His wrath. It is, however, the intention of God the Father for His children to become like Christ via the process of sanctification (Romans 8:29).

On this side of Heaven, full sanctification is unobtainable. The warning herein is to be careful about following the ways of the world after claiming Jesus as the Lord and Savior of one's life. This type of living is hypocritical and counterproductive to the cause of the gospel. When one claims to know Christ as his Savior yet continues to live in a manner contrary to his calling, he may be playing games with salvation. I believe one of the most powerful verses in the Bible is found in the book of Matthew, chapter seven, verse twenty-one: "Not everyone who says to me, 'Lord, Lord,' will enter the kingdom of heaven, but the one who does the will of my Father who is in heaven."

Mankind has grown weary of those who assert knowledge of ultimate truth and will not tolerate those who make such claims. While Jesus has paid the ultimate price for our real sin in full, becoming a servant of His will cost a follower something. Said cost is not necessarily monetary but certainly social.

"If the world hates you, remember that it hated Me before it hated you" (John 15:18). There is no greater joy, peace, or contentment than what one finds in the presence of the Almighty. My goal is not self-satisfaction; it is to glorify and honor Jesus (1 Peter 4:11; 1 Corinthians 10:31; et al.).[1]

THANK YOU FOR READING!

Thank you for reading *Question Everything*. If you found this book to be useful and informative, please tell your friends about it. Also, please consider posting a review on Amazon.com, BookBub.com, Goodreads.com, and/or wherever you buy your books, so that other readers will know if they would like to read it as well.

Dr. Walp is always open to respectable questions and comments, so please feel free to connect with him. You can find all his contact information and social media links on his website: www.AGWalp.com

ABOUT THE AUTHOR

Dr. A. G. Walp is the administrator of Payson Christian School in Payson, Arizona. He served the public for eleven years as a police officer in Florida and North Carolina. After making the rank of detective with the Charlotte-Mecklenburg Police Department in N.C., he retired from police work to enter the ministry. He holds an earned PhD in Higher Education Leadership, an earned Doctorate in Christian Apologetics from Southern Evangelical Seminary, an Education Specialist degree, a Masters in Pastoral Counseling, and an Undergraduate in Religion from Liberty University.

He and his wife of more than 34 years, T.J., have raised two sons and now have a beautiful granddaughter. Dr. Walp hated God until he was twenty-seven years old, but then he came to know the transcendent brilliance of God who also loves each and every one of us despite who we are and what we have done. He has been a guest speaker at schools, universities, churches, and special events and would love to talk with you, to get to know you, and to help you in any way he can. You can interact, ask questions, or send Dr. Walp a private message via one of the links below. (Education: Ph.D., D.Min., Ed.S., MAR, BS).

Dr. Walp is always open to respectable questions and comments, so please feel free to connect with him. You can find

all his contact information and social media links on his
website: www.AGWalp.com

in linkedin.com/in/agwalp
BB bookbub.com/authors/a-g-walp
▶ youtube.com/@backpacksouthwest

BIBLIOGRAPHY

Barna Group. available. www.barna.org/barna-update/article/16-teensnext-gen/147-most-twentysomethings-put-christianity-on-the-shelf-following-spiritually-active-teen-years [accessed October 5, 2011].

English Standard Bible. Wheaton, IL: Crossway Bibles, 2008.

[Staff?], comp. Voyager Spacecraft finds Solar System is Bigger than Thought. http://www.cnn.com/2012/12/03/us/space-voyager-solar-system/in-dex.html (accessed December 18, 2012).

Abbott, Lon, and Terri Cook. *Hiking the Grand Canyon's Geology*. Seattle: Mountaineers Books, 2004.

Alles, David L. *The Delta of the Colorado River*. Bellingham, WA: Western Washington University, 2007.

———. *The Delta of the Colorado River*. Bellingham, WA: Western Washington University, 2007.

Alles, The Delta of the Colorado River. *Introduction*.

Allis, David C., Thoms Jenuwein, and Danny Reinberg. *Epigenetics*. Cold Spring Harbor, NY: Cold Spring Harbor Laboratory Press, 2007.

Alroy, J. "The Shifting Balance of Diversity Among Major Marine Animal Groups." *Science* 329, no. 5996 (September-3-10).

Alt, David D. *Glacial Lake Missoula: And Its Humongous Floods*. Missoula, MT: Mountain Press Publishing, 201, n.d.

Andrew, A. Snelling, Thirtieth Anniversary of a Geologic Catastrophe, [Online], available. www.answersingenesis.org/articles/2010/05/18/thirti-eth-anniversary-of-geologic-catastrophe [accessed November 23, 2011].

Angelo, Joseph A. *Encyclopedia of Space and Astronomy*. New York: Infobase Publishing, 2006.

Anthony, M. *Changing Societies: Essential Sociology for Our Times*. Lanham, MD: Rowman & Littlefield Publishers,, 1999.

Archer, Gleason L. *Encyclopedia of Bible Difficulties*. Grand Rapids: Baker, 1982.

Armstrong, Herbert W. *Mystery of the Ages*. New York: Mead, 1985.

Asphaug, Erik. "The Small Planets." *Scientific American* 282 (May 2000).

Austin, Steve. *Grand Canyon*, 101-2. Santee, CA: Institute for Creation Research, 1994.

Avison, John. *The World of Physics*. Cheltenham, UK: Thomas Nelson and Sons, 1989.

Ayed, Ayeda, and Theodore Hup. *Molecular Biology Intelligence Unit.* New York: Springer Science & Business Media, LLC, 2010.

Balbus, Steven A. "A Powerful Local Shear Instability in Weakly Magnetized Disks." *Astrophysical Journal* 376, no. 214 (1991): 214-33.

Balchin, Jon. *Science: 100 Scientists Who Changed the World*, 62-63. New York: Enchanted Lion Books, 2003.

Barber, Nigel. "The Human Beast." *Psychology Today*, May 18, 2010.

———. Most Twentysomethings Put Christianity on the Shelf Following Spiritually Active Teen Years. http://www.barna.org/barna-update/article/16-teensnext-gen/147-most-

Bauer, Mary M. *The Truth about You.* Acton, MA: VanderWyk & Burnham, 2006.

Baxter, M. S., and A. Walton. "Fluctuations of Atmospheric Carbon-14 Concentrations during the Past Century." *Proceedings of the Royal Society of London* 321, no. 1544 (January 1971).

Behe, Michael J. *Darwin's Black Box.* New York: Free Press, 1996.

———. *Darwin's Black Box: The Biochemical Challenge to Evolution.* New York: Simon & Schuster, 1996.

Blanton, Dana. *Most Believe Prayer Heals.* 45% believe in Creationism, [Online], available:. www.foxnews.com/politics/2011/09/07/fox-news-poll-most-believe-prayer-heals-45-believe-in-creationism/?test=latestnews [accessed September 8, 2011].

Carl Sagan. Carl Sagan," NOVA, [Online], available. www.pbs.org/wgbh/nova/space/sagan-alien-abduction.html [accessed October 22, 2011].

Beckerman, Martin. *Molecular and Cellular Signaling.* New York: Springer Science + Business Media, 2005.

Berger. *Wiggles and Deviations" Proven by Historical and Archeological Means, " SAO/NASA.*

Berger, Rainer. "Suess.'" *Wiggles and Deviations" Proven by Historical and Archeological Means,"* SAO/NASA 20, no. 2 (June 1985).

Bertram, J. "The Molecular Biology of Cancer." *Molecular Aspects Medicine* 21, no. 6 (2000).

Billingsley, George H., and Susan S. Priest. "Geological Map of the House Rock Valley Area, Coconino County, Northern Arizona." *USGS: Science for a Changing World.*

Bodenheimer, Peter H. *Principles of Star Formation.* New York: Springer, 2011.

Bouw, G. "A Response to de Young's Ex Nihilo Article." *Bulletin of the Tychonian Society* 53 (1990).

Brown, Walter. *In the Beginning: Compelling Evidence for Creation and the Flood.* Phoenix: Center for Scientific Creation, 2001.

Budziszewski, J. *How to Stay Christian in College*. Colorado Springs: Think, 2004.

Butzer, Karl W. *Environment and Archeology*. Chicago: Aldine-Atherton, 1971.

Caputo, John D. "Kant's Refutation of the Cosmological Argument." *Journal of the American Academy of Religion* 79, no. 3 (December 1974).

Carroll, R. L. *Vertebrate Paleontology and Evolution*. New York: W. H. Freeman and, 1988.

Casey Laskin, Intelligent Design and the Origin of Biological Information: A Response to Dennis Venema [Online]. available. www.discovery.org/a/17571 [accessed November 7, 2011].

Chambers, John E. "Planetary Accretion in the Inner Solar System." *Science Direct* (April 2004).

Chisholm, B. S. *The Chemistry of Prehistoric Human Bone*. Cambridge: Cambridge University, 1989.

Cloud, John. "Why Your DNA Isn't Your Destiny." Time, *Wednesday*, January 6, 2010.

Colbert, E. H., and M. Morales. *Evolution of the Vertebrates*. New York: John Wiley and Sons, 1991.

Condie, K. C. *Plate Tectonics and Crustal Evolution*. Oxford: Butterworth-Heinemann, 1997.

Creagh, D. C., and David A. Bradley. *Radiation in Art and Archeometry*. Amsterdam: Elsevier Science B. V., 2000.

Cremo, Michael A., and Richard I. Thompson. *Forbidden Archeology: The Hidden History of the Human Race*. India: Bhaktivedanta, 1998.

Cuff, David J., and Andrew Goudie. *The Oxford Companion to Global Change*. Oxford: Oxford University Press, 2008.

Cuvier, George. *Essay on the Theory of the Earth*. Cambridge: Cambridge University Press-Blackwood, 1815 (2009 ed.

Darwin, Charles. *Insectivorous Plants*. New York: D. Appleton and Company, 1875.

———. *On the Origin of Species by Means of Natural Selection*. New York: D. Appleton and Company, 1861.

———. *The Origin of Species*. New York: Gramercy, 1979.

———. *The Origin of Species, 6th Edition*. New York: Macmillan Publishing, 1927.

Davis, Nicole. *Broad Institute Awarded Major Grant to Bolster Epigenomics Research*. [Online], available. www.broadinstitute.org/news/press-releases/1104 [accessed September 14, 2011].

Dawkins, Richard. *The Blind Watchmaker*. London: W.W. Norton, 1987.

———. *The God Delusion*. New York: First Mariner Books, 2006.

Dawson. *The Geology of Nova Scotia, New Brunswick and Prince Edward Island*, 94.233.

Dawson, John William. *The Geology of Nova Scotia, New Brunswick and Prince Edward Island*. Edinburgh, UK: MaCmillian and, 1891.

Day, Jeremy J, and J David Sweatt. *DNA Methylation and Memory Formation*. [Online], available. www.nature.com/neuro/journal/v13/n11/full/nn.2666.html [accessed September 16, 2011].

De Pater, Imke. *Planetary Sciences*. Cambridge: Cambridge University Press, 2010.

Dembski, William A. *Intelligent Design*. Downers Grove, IL: InterVaristy Press, 1999.

Dembski, William A., and Jonathan Wells. *The Design of Life*. Dallas: Foundation for Thought and Ethics, 2008.

DeYoung, Don. *Thousands Not Billions*. Portland: Master books, 2005.

———. *Thousands Not Billions: Challenging an Icon of Evolution, Questioning the Age of the Earth*. Portland: Master Books, 2005.

Doolittle, William E. Dendrochronology. http://uts.cc.utexas.edu/~wd/courses/373F/notes/lec20den.html (accessed August 31, 2012).

Edwards, Jonathan. *The Mind*. OR: University of Oregon, 1955.

Edwards, Ron, and Lisa Dickie. *Diamonds and Gemstones*, 10-14. New York: Crabtree Publishing Company, 2004.

Eldra Pearl Solomon et al. *Biology*. Belmont, CA: Brooks/Cole-Thomson Learning, 2005.

Elias et al. *Driver" Of Epidermal Pigmentation in Humans*.

Elias, Peter et al. "Barrier Requirements as the Evolutionary." *Driver" of Epidermal Pigmentation in Humans, "* American Journal of Human Biology 22, no. 4 (2010).

Elias, Peter, Gapinathan Menon, Bruce J Wetzel, and John W. Williams. "Barrier Requirements as the Evolutionary." *Driver" of Epidermal Pigmentation in Humans." American Journal of Human Biology* 22, no. 4 (2010): 526-37.

Elliott, Charles. *Delineation of Roman Catholicism: Drawn from the Authentic and Acknowledged Standards*, chap. XII.J. New York: George Lane, 1841.

Elson, John. "How Man Created God." *Time*, September 27, 1993.

Erickson, Jon. *Quakes, Eruptions, and Other Geologic Cataclysms: Revealing the Earth's Hazards*. New York: Facts on File, 2001.

Faulkner, Rebecca. *Geology Rocks*. Chicago: Raintree, 2008.

Ferguson-Smith, Anne C., John M. Greally, and Robert A. Martienssen, eds. Epigenomics (New York: Springer, 2009).

Fields, Helen. *Dinosaur Shocker*. n.p.: Smithsonian Magazine, 2006. www.smithsonianmag.com/science-nature/dinosaur.html [accessed November 23, 2011].

Fixsen, D. J. et al. "Cosmic Microwave Background Dipole Spectrum

Measured by the COBE FIRAS Instrument." *Astrophysical Journal* 420, no. 2 (1994).

Ford, Brian J. *Advances in Imaging and Electron Physics*. Amsterdam: Academic Press, 2009.

Forehand, M. *Bloom's Taxonomy:*. GA: University of Georgia, 2005.

Francis, Richard C. *The Ultimate Mystery of Inheritance: Epigenetics*. New York: W. W. Norton & Company, 2011.

Francis, The Ultimate Mystery of Inheritance. *Preface*.

Frater, George. *Our Humanist Heritage: A Handbook for Humanists*. Fairfax, VA: Xulon Press, 2010.

Frontieres, Atlantica Sequier. *Circumstellar Dust Disks and Planet Formation*. Gif sur Yvette Cedex- France: Editions Frontiers, 1994.

Geisler and Turek. *I Don't Have Enough Faith to Be an Atheist*, 74.

Geisler, Norman L. *Baker Encyclopedia of Christian Apologetics*. Grand Rapids: Zondervan, 1999.

———. *The Baker Encyclopedia of Christian Apologetics.*" Grand Rapids, MI: Baker Books, 1999.

Geisler, Norman L., and Paul K. Hoffman. *Why I Am a Christian: Leading Thinkers Explain Why They Believe*, 97-98. Grand Rapids: Baker Books, 2006.

Geisler, Norman, and Frank Turek. *I Don't Have Enough Faith to Be an Atheist*. Wheaton, IL: Crossway, 2004.

Geisler, Norman, and Ron Brooks. *When Skeptics Ask*, 26-29. Grand Rapids: Baker Books, 2001.

Geographic, National. *Global Warming Fast Facts*. [Online], available. news.-nationalgeographic.com/news/2004/12/1206_041206_global_warming.html [accessed September 28, 2011].

Gibson, Arthur. *God and the Universe*. New Fetter Lane London: Routledge, 2000.

Gills, James. *The Mysterious Epigenome*. 2011.

Gish, Duane T. *Evolution*. El Cajon, CA: Institute for Creation Research, 1995.

Gitt, Werner. *The Wonder of Man*. Bielefeld, Germany: Christliche Literatur-Verbreitung, 1999.

Glanzer, Perry L., and Todd C. Ream. *Christianity and Moral Identity in Higher Education*. New York: Palgrave Macmillian, 2009.

Glimm-Lacy, Janice, and Peter B. Kaufman. *Botany Illustrated: Introduction to Plants, Major Groups, Flowering Plant Families*. New York: Springer, 2006.

Goldberg, A. D., C. D. Allis, and E. Bernstein. "Epigenetics: A Landscape Takes Shape." *Cell* 128, no. 4 (February 2007).

Gould, Stephen J. *Rock of Ages*. NY: Ballantine Publishing Group, 1999.

Gradstein, Felix M., James G. Ogg, and Alan G. Smith, eds. *A Geologic Time Scale*. Cambridge: Cambridge University Press, 2005.

Gribbin, John. *In Search of the Big Bang: Quantum Physics and Cosmology*. New York: Bantam Books, 1986.

Guillermo, Gonzalez. *The Privileged Planet*. Washington, DC: Regency Publishing, 2004.

Gupta, Avijit. *Large Rivers: Geomorphology and Management*. West Sussex, England: John Wiley & Sons, 2007.

Habermas, Gary R., and Michael Licona. *The Case for the Resurrection*. Grand Rapids: Kregel, 2004.

Hal, Jonathan M. *A History of the Archaic Greek World*. Malden, MA: Blackwell, 2007.

Ham, Ken. *The New Answers Book 3*. Green Forest, AR: Master Books, 2009.

Ham, Ken, and Britt Beemer. *Already Gone*. Green Forest, AR: Master books, 2009.

Ham, Ken, Jonathan Sarfati, and Carl Wieland. *Did God Really Take Six Days?* Green Forest, AR: Masters Books, 2006.

Hans Volker Klapdor-Kleingrothaus. *Dark Matter in Astrophysics and Particle Physics, 1998*. Danvers, MA: IOP Publishing, 1999.

Hawking, Stephen. *The Beginning of Time*. [Online], available. http://www.hawking.org.uk/index.php/lectures/62 (accessed December 6, 2011).

———. *On the Shoulders of Giants*. Philadelphia: Running press, 2002.

Hellerman, Simeon, and Ian Swanson. *Dimension-Changing Exact Solutions of String Theory*. New York: Cornell University, 2006.

Hobday, Liz. *Scientists Accurately Date Earliest Human Fossil*. [Online], available. www.abc.net.au/am/content/2011/s3313709.htm [accessed September 9, 2011].

Hooke, Robert. *Microgrpahia: Or Some Physiological Depictions of Minute Bodies Made by Magnifying Glasses*. London: National Library of Medicine, 1665.

Hoyle, Fredrick, and Nalin Chandra Wickramasinghe. *Astronomical Origins of Life: Steps Towards Panspermia*. Dordrecht, Netherlands: Kluwer Academic Publishers, 2000.

Hubbard, L. Ron. *Clear Body, Clear Mind: The Effective Purification Program*. Los Angeles: Bridge Publishing, 2001.

Huddart, David, and Tim Stott. *Earth Environments: Past, Present, and Future*. West Susex, UK: John Wiley & Sons,, 2010.

Hutton, James. *The Theory of the Earth from the Transactions of the Royal Society of Edinburgh*. Paris: Royal Society of Edinburgh, 1788.

Jedicke, Peter. *SETI: The Search for Alien Intelligence*. North Mankato, MN: Byron Press Visual Publications, 2003.

Jessop, Carolyn, and Laura Palmer. *Escape*. New York: Broadway Books, 2007.

Jevremovic, Tatjana. *Nuclear Principles in Engineering*. New York: Springer, 2009.

Jirtle, Randy. *Epigenetics: Environmental Factors Can Alter the Way Our Genes Are Expressed*. NOVA transcript, July 24,. n.p.: NOVA, 2007.

Joesten, Melvin D., John L. Hogg, and Mary E. Castellion. *The World of Chemistry*. Belmont, CA: Thomson Brooks/Cole, 2007.

Johanson, Donald. *Lucy, the Beginnings of Humankind*. New York: Simon & Schuster, 1990.

Karam, Jose A. *Apoptosis in Carcinogenesis and Chemotherapy*. Netherlands: Springer, 2009.

Kearey, Philip. *Dictionary of Geology*. New York: Penguin Reference, 2001.

Kelly, Douglas, Philip B. Rollinson, and Frederick T. Marsh. *The Westminster Shorter Catechism in Modern English*. n.p.: Presbyterian and Reformed Pub., 1986.

King, Clarence. "Catastrophism and Evolution." *The American Naturalist* 11, no. 8 (August 1877).

Kitchener, Richard F. *The World View of Contemporary Physics: Does It Need a New Metaphysics?* Albany: State University of New York Press, 1988.

Koeberl, Christian, and Kenneth MacLeod, eds. *Catastrophic Events and Mass Extinctions: Impacts and Beyond, Issue 356*. Boulder, CO: Geological Society of America,, 2002.

Kotz, John C., Paul Treichel, and John Raymond Townsend. *Chemistry and Chemical Reactivity Vol. 2*. Belmont, CA: Cenage Learning, 2009.

Kreft, Peter. *The Handbook of Christian Apologetics*. Downers Grove, IL: InterVarsity Press, 1994.

Lamoureux, Scott. *Tracking Environmental Change Using Lake Sediments; Varve Chronology Techniques*. New York: Kluwer Academic, 2002.

Lang, Helen. *The Order of Nature in Aristotle's Physics*. Cambridge, UK: Cambridge, 1998.

Leclerc, Georges-Louis. *Natural History, General and Particular*. Bristol: Thoemmes Press, 2000.

Lecointre, Guillaume, and Herve Le Guyader. *The Tree of Life: A Phylogenetic Classification*. Harvard: President and Fellows of Harvard College, 2006.

Leddra, Michael. *Time Matters: Geology's Legacy to Scientific Thought*. West Sussex, UK: Willey-Blackwell, 2010.

Lee, Stan. "Spider-Man." *Columbia Pictures*.

Leventhal, Barry. *Class Discussion*. Matthews, NC: Southern Evangelical Seminary, January 6, 2012.

Levin, Simon A. *Encyclopedia of Biodiversity, Volume 2*. Salt Lake City: Academic Press, 2001.

Libby, W. "Radiocarbon Dating, Memories, and Hopes." *Proceedings of the*

Eighth International Radiocarbon Dating Conference 1, no. 721019 (October 1972).

Lisa Randall, Knocking on Heaven's Door: How Physics and Scientific Thinking Illuminate the Universe and the Modern World (New York: Harper Collins, 2011), sec. V. 2011).

Lodish, H. et al. *Molecular Biology of the Cell 5th Edition*. New York: WH Freeman, 2004.

Lowe, D. C. "Problems Associated with the Use of Coal as a Source of 14C Free Background Material." *Radiocarbon* 31, no. 2 (1989).

Lujan, Michael L. *Master Instructional Strategies*. Tyler, TX: Mentoring Minds, 2008.

Lyell, Charles. *Principles of Geology: An Attempt to Explain the Former Changes of the Earth's Surface, by Reference to Causes Now in Operation.* Cambridge: Cambridge University Press, 2009.

Malainey, Mary E. *A Consumer's Guide to Archaeological Science: Analytical Techniques*. New York: Springer, 2010.

———. *A Consumer's Guide to Archaeological Science: Analytical Techniques*. New York: Springer, 2010.

Martin. *Flood Legends: Global Clues of a Common Event*, chap. 1.

Martin, Charles. *Flood Legends: Global Clues of a Common Event*. Green Forest, AR: Master Books, 2009.

Marvel, Kevin B. *Astronomy Made Simple*. New York: Broadway Books, 2004.

Mathez, Edmond A. *Earth: Inside and Out*. New York: New Press, 2000.

McaKee, Edwin D., and Charles E. Resser. *Cambrian History of the Grand Canyon Region*. Baltimore: Lord Baltimore Press, 1945.

McArthur, John. *John McArthur Study Bible*. Nashville: Thomas Nelson, 1997.

McDowell, Josh. *The Best of Josh McDowell*. Atlanta: Thomas Nelson, 1993.

———. *Evidence That Demands a Verdict*. Nashville: Thomas Nelson, 2005.

McDowell, Sean. *Apologetics for a New Generation*. Eugene, OR: Harvest House, 2009.

McIntyre, D. B., and Alan McKirdy. *James Hutton: The Founder of Modern Geology*. Edinburgh, UK: National Museums of Scotland Pub., 2001.

McNeese, Tim. *The Colorado River*. Broomall, PA: Chelsea House Publishers, 2004.

Meyer, Stephen C. "The Origin of Biological Information and the Higher Taxonomic Categories." *Proceedings of the Biological Society of Washington* 117, no. 2 (2004).

Miglani, Gurbachan S. *Developmental Genetics*. New Delhi: I.K. International Publishing House, 2006.

Miller. "The Seductive Allure of Behavioral Epigenetics." *Science*, July, 2010.

Milligan, Mark. *How Do Geologists Know How Old a Rock Is?* [Online], available. geology.utah.gov/surveynotes/gladasked/gladage.htm [accessed November 25, 2011].

Milton Karl Munitz. *Theories of the Universe: From Babylonian Myth to Modern Science.* New York: Free Press, 1957.

Morris, John. *Footprints in the Ash.* Green Forest, AR: Master Books, 2005.

—— D. "The Polystrate Trees and Coal Seams of Joggins Fossil Cliffs." *Impact,* no. 316 (1999).

Morris, Leon. *The Expositor's Bible Commentary.* Grand Rapids: Zondervan, 1981.

Morrow, Jonathan. *Welcome to College: A Christ-Follower's Guide for the Journey.* Grand Rapids: Kregel Publications, 2008.

NASA, Dark Energy. available. science.nasa.gov/astrophysics/focus-areas/what-is-dark-energy/ [accessed December 2, 2011].

National Park Service, Grand Canyon: Nature and Science [Online]. available. http://www.nps.gov/grca/naturescience/index.htm (accessed December 9, 2011).

National Research Council (US) Committee on the Physics of the Universe, comp. and ed. *Connecting Quarks with the Cosmos: Eleven Science Questions for the New Century.* Washington, DC: National Academic Press, 2003.

Nave, Carl R. *Carbon Dating.* Atlanta: Georgia State University, 2001.

Nevid, Jeffrey S. *Psychology: Concepts and Applications.* Boston: Houghton Mifflin Company, 2009.

Newberg, Andrew B., and G. Eugene. *Why God Won't Go Away (New York: Ballantine Books, 2002). Richard Dawkins, the God Delusion.* Boston: Mariner books, 2008.

Nobel. *Physicochemical and Environmental Plant Physiology,* 410.

Nobel, Park S. *Physicochemical and Environmental Plant Physiology: 4th Ed.* Burlington, MA: Academic Press, 2009.

Norman Meek and John Douglass, Lake Overflow: An Alternative Hypothesis for Grand Canyon Incision and Development of the Colorado River [Online]. available at. http://geomorphology.sese.asu.edu/Papers/31-lake_overflow-an_alternative_hypothesis.pdf (accessed December 11, 2011).

NOVA, Epigenetics. available. www.pbs.org/wgbh/nova/body/epigenetics.html [accessed September 28, 2011].

O'Reilly. *Grand Canyon,* 26.

Palla, F. *Physics of Star Formation in Galaxies.* New York: Springer, 2002.

Papantonopoulos, Eleftherios. *The Invisible Universe: Dark Matter and Dark Energy.* Athens, Greece: Springer, 2007.

Park, R., and S. Epstein. "Carbon Isotope Fractionation during Photosynthesis." *Geochim* 4090750 (December 2009).

Parker, Gary. *Creation: Facts of Life*. Green Forest, AR: Master Books, 2006.

Parry, Wynne. Science Vs God: Does Progress Trump Faith? http://www.-foxnews.com/science/2012/12/07/science-vs-god-does-progress-trump-faith/ (accessed December 24, 2012).

Parsons, A. J., and Athol D. Abrahams. *Geomorphology of Desert Environments*. Dordrecht, Netherlands: Springer Science + Business Media, 2009.

Pasquini, John J. *The Existence of God: Convincing and Converging Arguments*. Lanham, Md: University Press of America,, 2010.

Patterson, Roger. *Evolution Exposed*. Petersburg, KY: Answers in Genesis, 2006.

Petronis, Arthuras, and Jonathan Mill, eds. *Brain, Behavior and Epigenetics*. New York: Springer-, 2011.

Phillips, Melanie. *The World Turned Upside Down: Global Battle Over God, Truth, and Power*. New York: Encounter Books, 2010.

Potter, Douglas. *Developing a Christian Apologetics Educational Program in the Secondary School*. Eugene, OR: Wipf & Stock, 2010.

———. *Response as Primary Reader to This Ministry Project*. Matthews, NC: Southern Evangelical Seminary, 2012.

Rafferty, John P., ed. *Geological Sciences*. New York: Britannica Educational Publishing, 2012.

Raham, Gary. *The Restless Earth: Fossils*. New York: Infobase Publishing, 2009.

Rainbolt, George W., and Sandra L. Dwyer. *Critical Thinking: The Art of Argument*. Boston: Wadsworth, 2012.

Rajca, John. "Keys to Rapid Rock Formation." *Creation*, December, 1994.

Rampelotto, P. H. "Panspermia: A Promising Field of Research." *The Smithsonian/NASA Astrophysics Data System*, no. 1538 (April 2010).

Randall, Lisa. *Knocking on Heaven's Door*, 370-71. New York: Harper Collins Publishers, 2011.

Ranney, Wayne. *Carving Grand Canyon: Evidence, Theories, and Mystery*. Grand Canyon: Grand Canyon Association, 2005.

Rapp, Donald. *Ice Ages and Interglacials: Measurements, Interpretation and Models*. New York: Springer, 2009.

Razavy, Mohsen. *Quantum Theory of Tunneling*. Singapore: World Scientific Publishing, 2003.

Reger, Daniel L., Scott R. Goode, and David W. Ball. *Chemistry: Principles and Practice*. Belmont, CA: Cengage Learning, 2009.

Regnerus, Mark D., and Jeremy E. Uecker. *How Corrosive Is College to Religious Faith and Practice?* New York: Social Science Research Council, 2007.

Reichenbach, Bruce R. *The Cosmological Argument*. Springfield: Charles Thomas, 1972.

Reipurth, Bo, DAvid Jewitt, and Klaus Keil. *Protostars and Planets V, Volume 5*. Tucson: University of Arizona Press, 2007.

Rhodes, Ron. *Answering the Objections of Atheists, Agnostics, & Skeptics*. Eugene, OR: Harvest House, 2006.

Ribokas, Bob. *Grand Canyon Explorer*. 753, [Online], available at. http://www.bobspixels.com/kaibab.org/misc/gc_coriv.htm   (accessed December 11, 2011).

———. *Grand Canyon Explorer*. 753, [Online], available at. http://www.bobspixels.com/kaibab.org/misc/gc_coriv.htm (accessed December 11, 2011).

Robert, J. Marzano, and John S. Kendall. *The New Taxonomy of Educational Objectives*. Thousand Oak, CA: Corwin Press, 2007.

Rogers, Kara. *The 100 Most Influential Scientists of All Time*. New York: Britannica Educational Publishing, 2010.

Rohde, R. A., and R. A. Muller. "Cycles in Fossil Diversity." *Nature*.

Rolando Del Carmon. *Black's Law Dictionary*. Mason, Ohio: Thomson West, 2006.

Ross, Hugh. *A Matter of Days: Resolving a Creation Controversy*. Colorado Springs: NavPress, 2004.

Ross, Hugh, and Gleason Archer. *The G3n3s1s Debate*. Mission Viejo, CA: Cruxpress, 2001.

Rudwick, Martin J. S. *Georges Cuvier, Fossil Bones, and Geologic Catastrophes*. Chicago: University of Chicago Press, 1997.

Russell, Peter J., Paul E. Hertz, and Beverely McMillian. *Biology: The Dynamic Science (Second Edition)*. Belmont, CA: Brooks Cole, 2008.

Sadava, David, Heller Hillis, and Berenbaum, eds. *Life: The Science of Biology 9th Edition*. S, n.d.

Sadava, Heller, Purves Orains, and .,. Hillis, comps. and eds. *Life: The Science of Biology 8th Edition*. S, n.d.

Sanderson, Stephen K. "Adaptation, Evolution, and Religion." *Religion* 38, no. 2 (June 2008).

Sapp, Jan. *Genesis: Molecular Biology and Organismic Complexity*. Oxford: Oxford University Press, 2003.

Schilling, Govert. *Atlas of Astronomical Discoveries*. New York: Springer, 2008.

Scott, Eugenie C.. "The Creation/Evolution Continuum." *Reports of the National Center for Science*.

Shaw, Ron. *Great Scientists and Discoveries*. Carlton South Vic, Australia: Curriculum Press, 2003.

Slee. *Slee's Health Care Terms 5th Ed.*

Slee, Deborah A., and Vergil N. Slee. *Slee's Health Care Terms 5th Ed.* Sudbury, MA: Jones and Bartlett, 2008.

Slick, Matthew. Contradictions in Watchtower Literature. http://carm.org/con-
tradictions-in-watchtower-literature (accessed March 2, 2012).

Smith, Christian, and Melinda Lundquist Denton. *Soul Searching: The Religious and Spiritual Lives of American Teenagers*. United Kingdom: Oxford
Univsersity Press, 2005.

Spetner, Lee M. *Not by Chance*. New York: Judaica Press, 1998.

Stagiritis, Aristotle. *Aristotle's Ethics as First Philosophy*. Cambridge, NY:
Cambridge, 2008.

Starr, Cecie et al. *Biology: The Unity and Diversity of Life*. Belmont, CA:
Cengage Learning, 2009.

Stillman, Bruce. *Epigenetics: Symposia on Quantitative Biology*. Cold Springs
Harbor, NY: Cold Springs Harbor Laboratory Press, 2004.

Stokes, Jerry. *Mormonism 2010 Handbook on Mormonism*, 20-205. Newberg,
OR: Chehalem Valley Baptist Church, 2008.

Story, Dan. *Engaging the Closed Minded: Presenting Your Faith to the
Confirmed Unbeliever*. Grand Rapids: Kregel Pub., 1999.

Stott, Carole et al., ed. *Space: From Earth to the Edge of the Universe*. New
York: DK, 2010.

Strobel, Lee. *The Case for a Creator*. Grand Rapids: Zondervan, 2004.

Strong, James. *The Exhaustive Concordance of the Bible*. Peabody, MA:
Hendrickson Publishing, 1988.

Swiggum, S., and M. Kohli, comps. *Wreck of the Isabella Watson*. [Online],
available.   http://www.theshipslist.com/ships/Wrecks/isabellawat-
son1852.htm (accessed October 26, 2011).

Swinton, W. E. *Biology and Comparative Physiology for Birds*. New York:
Academic Press, 1960.

Tamers, M.A., and D.G. Hood. *Radiocarbon Sample Data Sheet*. [Online],
available.   www.radiocarbon.com/PDF/Beta-Analytic-Data-Sheet.pdf
[accessed September 28, 2011].

Thoresen, Carl E. "Spirituality and Health: Is There a Relationship." *Journal
of Health Psychology* 4, no. 3 (May 1999).

Tilak, Avanti. *Constraints on Jets and Accretion Disks in Low Luminosity
Radio Galaxies*. Harvard: Harvard University, 2006.

Tobin, Allan J., and Jennie Dusheck. *Ask about Life*. Belmont, CA:
Brooks/Cole-Thomson Learning, 2005.

Todhunter, Isaac, William Whewell, and Richard Yeo. *William Whewell: An
Account of His Writing with Selections from His Literary and Scientific
Correspondence*. New York: Thoemmes Press, 2001.

Toriello, James. *The Human Genome Project*. New York: Rosen Publishing
Group, 2003.

U. S. Government employees, National Human Genome Research Institute,

[Online], available. doi:www.genome.gov/12011239 [accessed September 28, 2011].

University of Chicago Department of Geology. "New Erosion Cycle in Grand Canyon District." *The Journal of Geology* 18 (December 1910): 753.

Unk. "Bell-ieve It:: Rapid Rock Formation Rings True." *Creation* 20, no. 2 (March 1998): 6.

Van Der Plicht, Johannes. "The Groningen Radiocarbon Calibration Program." *Radiocarbon* 35, no. 1 (1993).

Wald, George. "The Origin of Life." *Scientific American* 191 (August 1954).

Walker, Mike. *Quaternary Dating Methods*. Chichester, West Sussex: John Wiley & Sons,, 2005.

——— J. *Quaternary Dating Methods*. West Sussex: John Wiley & Sons, 2005.

Wayne, R. Spencer, Can We See Stars Forming?, [Online], available. http://www.answersingenesis.org/articles/aid/v3/n1/star-formation-and-creation (accessed December 7, 2011).

Whitcomb, John C. "Progressive Creationism." *Impact*, no. 360 (June 2003).

Whitmeyer, Steven J., David W. Mogk, and Eric J. Pyle, eds. *Field Geology Education: Historical Perspectives and Modern Approaches*. Boulder: Geological Society of America, 2009.

Wicander and Monroe. *Historical Geology, 98*.

Wicander, Reed. *The Changing Earth: Exploring Geology and Evolution 5th Edition*. Belmont, CA: Cenage Learning, 2009.

Wicander, Reed, and James S. Monroe. *Historical Geology: Evolution of Earth and Life Through Time*. Belmont, CA: Cengage Learning, 2009.

Wiebe, Garth. *The Parable of the Candle*. [Online], available. http://www.answersingenesis.org/articles/1998/05/21/candle-parable (accessed January 7, 2012).

William Lane Craig. *The Existence of God and the Beginning of the Universe*. San Bernardino: Here's Life, 1979.

Wise, Kurt. *Faith, Form and Time: What the Bible Teaches and Science Confirms about Cration Adn the Age of the Universe*. 90: Boradman & Holdman, 2002.

Woodmorappe, John. "The Geologic Column: Does It Exist?" *Technical Journal* 13, no. 2 (November 1999).

Woodruff, David S. "Evolution: The Paleobioilogical View." *Science* 208, no. 16 (May 1980).

Wootton, R. J. *Biomechanics and the Origin of Insect Flight*. Cambridge: Cambridge, 1991.

Zuckerman, P. *Atheism: Contemporary Numbers and Patterns*. Cambridge: Cambridge University Press, 2007.

NOTES

PREFACE

1. Andrew B. Newberg and G. Eugene, *Why God Won't Go Away* (New York: Ballantine Books, 2002). *Richard Dawkins, the God Delusion* (Boston: Mariner books, 2008).

2. Ken Ham and Britt Beemer, *Already Gone* (Green Forest, AR: Master books, 2009).

3. Barna Group, available, www.barna.org/barna-update/article/16-teens-next-gen/147-most-twentysomethings-put-christianity-on-the-shelf-following-spiritually-active-teen-years [accessed October 5, 2011].

4. Christian Smith and Melinda Lundquist Denton, *Soul Searching: The Religious and Spiritual Lives of American Teenagers* (United Kingdom: Oxford Univsersity Press, 2005), 6.

5. Jonathan Morrow, *Welcome to College: A Christ-Follower's Guide for the Journey* (Grand Rapids: Kregel Publications, 2008), 1.

6. J. Budziszewski, *How to Stay Christian in College* (Colorado Springs: Think, 2004), 1.

7. Perry L. Glanzer and Todd C. Ream, *Christianity and Moral Identity in Higher Education* (New York: Palgrave Macmillian, 2009), 1.

8. Mark D. Regnerus and Jeremy E. Uecker, *How Corrosive Is College to Religious Faith and Practice?* (New York: Social Science Research Council, 2007).

9. Douglas Potter, *Developing a Christian Apologetics Educational Program in the Secondary School* (Eugene, OR: Wipf & Stock, 2010), Appendix.

10. Ham and Beemer, *Already Gone*.

11. Norman L. Geisler, *The Baker Encyclopedia of Christian Apologetics "* (Grand Rapids, MI: Baker Books, 1999).

12. Jonathan Edwards, *The Mind* (OR: University of Oregon, 1955).

13. L. Ron Hubbard, *Clear Body, Clear Mind: The Effective Purification Program* (Los Angeles: Bridge Publishing, 2001).

14. Carolyn Jessop and Laura Palmer, *Escape* (New York: Broadway Books, 2007).

15. Matthew Slick, Contradictions in Watchtower Literature, [Online], available, http://carm.org/contradictions-in-watchtower-literature (accessed March 2, 2012).

1. NATURAL DOUBTS

1. Jerry Stokes, *Mormonism 2010 Handbook on Mormonism* (Newberg, OR: Chehalem Valley Baptist Church, 2008).
2. *Carl Sagan*, Carl Sagan," NOVA", [Online], available, www.pbs.org/wgbh/nova/space/sagan-alien-abduction.html [accessed October 22, 2011].
3. Charles Martin, *Flood Legends: Global Clues of a Common Event* (Green Forest, AR: Master Books, 2009), 9.
4. Stephen Hawking, *On the Shoulders of Giants* (Philadelphia: Running press, 2002), 731.
5. Leon Morris, *The Expositor's Bible Commentary* (Grand Rapids: Zondervan, 1981), 113.
6. Rolando Del Carmon, *Black's Law Dictionary* (Mason, Ohio: Thomson West, 2006).
7. Morris, *The Expositor's Bible Commentary*, 113.
8. Rolando Del Carmon, *Black's Law Dictionary*.
9. Josh McDowell, *Evidence That Demands a Verdict* (Nashville: Thomas Nelson, 2005).

2. GOD'S EXISTENCE

1. P. Zuckerman, *Atheism: Contemporary Numbers and Patterns* (Cambridge: Cambridge University Press, 2007).
2. Nigel Barber, "The Human Beast," *Psychology Today*, May 18, 2010.
3. Stephen K. Sanderson, "Adaptation, Evolution, and Religion," *Religion* 38, no. 2 (June 2008).
4. Barber, "The Human Beast."
5. John Elson, "How Man Created God," *Time*, September 27, 1993.
6. Newberg and Eugene, *Why God Won't Go Away* (New York: Ballantine Books, 2002). *Richard Dawkins, the God Delusion*.
7. Elson, "How Man Created God."
8. Aristotle Stagiritis, *Aristotle's Ethics as First Philosophy* (Cambridge, NY: Cambridge, 2008).
9. Norman L. Geisler and Paul K. Hoffman, *Why I Am a Christian: Leading Thinkers Explain Why They Believe* (Grand Rapids: Baker Books, 2006).
10. Ibid.
11. Helen Lang, *The Order of Nature in Aristotle's Physics* (Cambridge, UK: Cambridge, 1998).
12. Geisler and Turek, *I Don't Have Enough Faith to Be an Atheist*.
13. John D. Caputo, "Kant's Refutation of the Cosmological Argument," *Journal of the American Academy of Religion* 79, no. 3 (December 1974).

14. John J. Pasquini, *The Existence of God: Convincing and Converging Arguments* (Lanham, Md: University Press of America,, 2010), 9.

15. Bruce R. Reichenbach, *The Cosmological Argument* (Springfield: Charles Thomas, 1972).

16. Kurt Wise, *Faith, Form and Time: What the Bible Teaches and Science Confirms about Creation and the Age of the Universe* (90: Boradman & Holdman, 2002).

17. D. J. Fixsen et al., "Cosmic Microwave Background Dipole Spectrum Measured by the COBE FIRAS Instrument," *Astrophysical Journal* 420, no. 2 (1994).

18. Thomas H. Maugh, "Relics of Big Bang, Seen for First Time," *Los Angeles Times*, April 24, 1992, under "A1; A30."

19. Norman Geisler and Ron Brooks, *When Skeptics Ask* (Grand Rapids: Baker Books, 2001).

3. THE GEOLOGIC COLUMN

1. Wicander and Monroe, *Historical Geology*, 98.

2. Wynne Parry, Science Vs God: Does Progress Trump Faith?, http://www.foxnews.com/science/2012/12/07/science-vs-god-does-progress-trump-faith/ (accessed December 24, 2012).

3. John Woodmorappe, "The Geologic Column: Does It Exist?," *Technical Journal* 13, no. 2 (November 1999).

4. Nave, *Carbon Dating*.

5. Edmond A. Mathez, *Earth: Inside and Out* (New York: New Press, 2000).

6. Ibid.

7. M.A. Tamers and D.G. Hood, *Radiocarbon Sample Data Sheet*, [Online], available, www.radiocarbon.com/PDF/Beta-Analytic-Data-Sheet.pdf [accessed September 28, 2011].

8. Mathez, *Earth: Inside and Out*.

9. K. C. Condie, *Plate Tectonics and Crustal Evolution* (Oxford: Butterworth-Heinemann, 1997).

10. Michael Leddra, *Time Matters: Geology's Legacy to Scientific Thought* (West Sussex, UK: Willey-Blackwell, 2010), 4.

11. John P. Rafferty, ed., *Geological Sciences* (New York: Britannica Educational Publishing, 2012).

12. Clarence King, "Catastrophism and Evolution," *The American Naturalist* 11, no. 8 (August 1877).

13. Rafferty, *Geological Sciences*.

14. George Cuvier, *Essay on the Theory of the Earth*, Cambridge: Cambridge university press-blackwood, 1815 (2009 ed.

15. Martin J. S. Rudwick, *Georges Cuvier, Fossil Bones, and Geologic Catastrophes* (Chicago: University of Chicago Press, 1997).

16. Philip Kearey, *Dictionary of Geology* (New York: Penguin Reference, 2001), 123.

17. D. B. McIntyre and Alan McKirdy, *James Hutton: The Founder of Modern Geology* (Edinburgh, UK: National Museums of Scotland Pub., 2001).

18. James Hutton, *The Theory of the Earth from the Transactions of the Royal Society of Edinburgh* (Paris: Royal Society of Edinburgh, 1788).

19. McIntyre and McKirdy, *James Hutton: The Founder of Modern Geology*.

20. Steven J. Whitmeyer, David W. Mogk, and Eric J. Pyle, eds., *Field Geology Education: Historical Perspectives and Modern Approaches* (Boulder: Geological Society of America, 2009), 228.

21. McIntyre and McKirdy, *James Hutton: The Founder of Modern Geology*.

22. Charles Lyell, *Principles of Geology: An Attempt to Explain the Former Changes of the Earth's Surface, by Reference to Causes Now in Operation* (Cambridge: Cambridge University Press, 2009).

23. Georges-Louis Leclerc, *Natural History, General and Particular* (Bristol: Thoemmes Press, 2000).

24. Isaac Todhunter, William Whewell, and Richard Yeo, *William Whewell: An Account of His Writing with Selections from His Literary and Scientific Correspondence* (New York: Thoemmes Press, 2001).

25. Leclerc, *Natural History, General and Particular*.

26. Roger Patterson, *Evolution Exposed* (Petersburg, KY: Answers in Genesis, 2006), chap. 4.

27. Rebecca Faulkner, *Geology Rocks* (Chicago: Raintree, 2008).

28. National Geographic, *Global Warming Fast Facts*, [Online], available, news.nationalgeographic.com/news/2004/12/1206_041206_global_warming.html [accessed September 28, 2011].

29. Gary Parker, *Creation: Facts of Life* (Green Forest, AR: Master Books, 2006).

30. John Rajca, "Keys to Rapid Rock Formation," *Creation*, December, 1994, 45.

31. S. Swiggum and M. Kohli, comps., *Wreck of the Isabella Watson*, [Online], available, http://www.theshipslist.com/ships/Wrecks/isabellawatson1852.htm (accessed October 26, 2011).

32. Unk, "Bell-ieve It:: Rapid Rock Formation Rings True," *Creation* 20, no. 2 (March 1998).

33. Michael A. Cremo and Richard I. Thompson, *Forbidden Archeology: The Hidden History of the Human Race* (India: Bhaktivedanta, 1998).

34. David Huddart and Tim Stott, *Earth Environments: Past, Present, and Future* (West Susex, UK: John Wiley & Sons,, 2010).

35. John William Dawson, *The Geology of Nova Scotia, New Brunswick and Prince Edward Island* (Edinburgh, UK: MaCmillian and, 1891), 233.

36. Brown, *In the Beginning*, 93.

37. Dawson, *The Geology of Nova Scotia, New Brunswick and Prince Edward Island.*

38. Charles Darwin, *The Origin of Species, 6th Edition* (New York: Macmillan Publishing, 1927), 322.

39. David S. Woodruff, "Evolution: The Paleobioilogical View," *Science* 208, no. 16 (May 1980): 716.

40. Eldra Pearl Solomon et al., *Biology* (Belmont, CA: Brooks/Cole-Thomson Learning, 2005), 341.

41. Allan J. Tobin and Jennie Dusheck, *Ask about Life* (Belmont, CA: Brooks/Cole-Thomson Learning, 2005), 361.

42. Charles Darwin, *On the Origin of Species by Means of Natural Selection* (New York: D. Appleton and Company, 1861), 265.

43. Richard Dawkins, *The Blind Watchmaker* (London: W.W. Norton, 1987), 229.

44. George Frater, *Our Humanist Heritage: A Handbook for Humanists* (Fairfax, VA: Xulon Press, 2010), 76.

45. Helen Fields, *Dinosaur Shocker* (n.p.: Smithsonian Magazine, 2006), www.smithsonianmag.com/science-nature/dinosaur.html   [accessed November 23, 2011].

46. Robert Lee Hotz, "Soft Tissue Discovered in Bone of a Dinosaur," *Los Angeles Times*, March 25, 2005, under "The Nation."

47. John D. Morris, "The Polystrate Trees and Coal Seams of Joggins Fossil Cliffs," *Impact*, no. 316 (1999).

48. A. Andrew, Snelling, Thirtieth Anniversary of a Geologic Catastrophe, [Online], available, www.answersingenesis.org/articles/2010/05/18/thirtieth-anniversary-of-geologic-catastrophe [accessed November 23, 2011].

49. Mark Milligan, *How Do Geologists Know How Old a Rock Is?*, [Online], available, geology.utah.gov/surveynotes/gladasked/gladage.htm [accessed November 25, 2011].

4. FOSSILS

1. Gary Raham, *The Restless Earth: Fossils* (New York: Infobase Publishing, 2009).

2. Simon A. Levin, *Encyclopedia of Biodiversity, Volume 2* (Salt Lake City: Academic Press, 2001).

3. George W. Rainbolt and Sandra L. Dwyer, *Critical Thinking: The Art of Argument* (Boston: Wadsworth, 2012).

4. Felix M. Gradstein, James G. Ogg, and Alan G. Smith, eds., *A Geologic Time Scale* (Cambridge: Cambridge University Press, 2005).

5. Rainbolt and Dwyer, *Critical Thinking: The Art of Argument.*

6. R. A. Rohde and R. A. Muller, "Cycles in Fossil Diversity," *Nature*.

7. Christian Koeberl and Kenneth MacLeod, eds., *Catastrophic Events and Mass Extinctions: Impacts and Beyond, Issue* 356 (Boulder, CO: Geological Society of America,, 2002).

8. Guillaume Lecointre and Herve Le Guyader, *The Tree of Life: A Phylogenetic Classification* (Harvard: President and Fellows of Harvard College, 2006).

9. Heller Sadava, Purves Orains, and .,. Hillis, comps. and eds., *Life: The Science of Biology 8th Edition* (S, n.d.), land, MA: Sinauer Associates, 2008), 12..

10. J. Alroy, "The Shifting Balance of Diversity Among Major Marine Animal Groups," *Science* 329, no. 5996 (September-3-10).

11. Duane T. Gish, *Evolution* (El Cajon, CA: Institute for Creation Research, 1995).

12. William A. Dembski and Jonathan Wells, *The Design of Life* (Dallas: Foundation for Thought and Ethics, 2008), 61.

13. R. J. Wootton, *Biomechanics and the Origin of Insect Flight* (Cambridge: Cambridge, 1991), 99.

14. George Wald, "The Origin of Life," *Scientific American* 191 (August 1954).

15. R. L. Carroll, *Vertebrate Paleontology and Evolution* (New York: W. H. Freeman and, 1988), 180.

16. E. H. Colbert and M. Morales, *Evolution of the Vertebrates* (New York: John Wiley and Sons, 1991), 223.

17. W. E. Swinton, *Biology and Comparative Physiology for Birds* (New York: Academic Press, 1960), 1.

18. Peter Elias et al., "Barrier Requirements as the Evolutionary," *Driver"* of *Epidermal Pigmentation in Humans, "* American Journal of Human Biology 22, no. 4 (2010).

19. Gish, *Evolution.*

20. Ibid.

21. H. Lodish et al., *Molecular Biology of the Cell 5th Edition* (New York: WH Freeman, 2004), 963.

22. Ibid.

23. Gish, *Evolution.*

5. THE GRAND CANYON

1. Brown, *In the Beginning.*

2. Ibid.

3. National Park Service, Grand Canyon: Nature and Science, *Available.*

4. John Morris, *Footprints in the Ash* (Green Forest, AR: Master Books, 2005).

5. Ken Ham, *The New Answers Book* 3 (Green Forest, AR: Master Books, 2009), 180.

6. A. J. Parsons and Athol D. Abrahams, *Geomorphology of Desert Environments* (Dordrecht, Netherlands: Springer Science + Business Media, 2009), 22.

7. Edwin D. McaKee and Charles E. Resser, *Cambrian History of the Grand Canyon Region* (Baltimore: Lord Baltimore Press, 1945), 122.

8. George H. Billingsley and Susan S. Priest, "Geological Map of the House Rock Valley Area, Coconino County, Northern Arizona," *USGS: Science for a Changing World*.

9. Steve Austin, *Grand Canyon* (Santee, CA: Institute for Creation Research, 1994).

10. Avijit Gupta, *Large Rivers: Geomorphology and Management* (West Sussex, England: John Wiley & Sons, 2007), 6.

11. David L. Alles, *The Delta of the Colorado River* (Bellingham, WA: Western Washington University, 2007).

12. O'Reilly, *Grand Canyon*.

13. Alles, *The Delta of the Colorado River*.

14. University of Chicago Department of Geology, "New Erosion Cycle in Grand Canyon District," *The Journal of Geology* 18 (December 1910).

15. Ibid.

16. Brown, *In the Beginning*.

17. Lon Abbott and Terri Cook, *Hiking the Grand Canyon's Geology* (Seattle: Mountaineers Books, 2004).

18. Bob Ribokas, *Grand Canyon Explorer*, 753, [Online], available at, http://www.bobspixels.com/kaibab.org/misc/gc_coriv.htm (accessed December 11, 2011).

19. Tim McNeese, *The Colorado River* (Broomall, PA: Chelsea House Publishers, 2004), chap. 1.

20. Wayne Ranney, *Carving Grand Canyon: Evidence, Theories, and Mystery* (Grand Canyon: Grand Canyon Association, 2005).

21. Norman Meek and John Douglass, Lake Overflow: An Alternative Hypothesis for Grand Canyon Incision and Development of the Colorado River [Online], available at, http://geomorphology.sese.asu.edu/Papers/31-lake_overflow-an_alternative_hypothesis.pdf (accessed December 11, 2011).

22. Norman Meek and John Douglass, Lake Overflow: An Alternative Hypothesis for Grand Canyon Incision and Development of the Colorado River [Online], available at, http://geomorphology.sese.asu.edu/Papers/31-lake_overflow-an_alternative_hypothesis.pdf (accessed December 11, 2011).

23. Brown, *In the Beginning*.

24. Martin, *Flood Legends: Global Clues of a Common Event*.

25. Brown, *In the Beginning*.

26. Jon Erickson, *Quakes, Eruptions, and Other Geologic Cataclysms: Revealing the Earth's Hazards* (New York: Facts on File, 2001), 86.

27. Brown, *In the Beginning.*

28. David D. Alt, *Glacial Lake Missoula: And Its Humongous Floods* (Missoula, MT: Mountain Press Publishing, 201, n.d.).

29. Donald Rapp, *Ice Ages and Interglacials: Measurements, Interpretation and Models* (New York: Springer, 2009).

6. RADIOMETRIC DATING

1. Liz Hobday, *Scientists Accurately Date Earliest Human Fossil,* [Online], available, www.abc.net.au/am/content/2011/s3313709.htm [accessed September 9, 2011].

2. Donald Johanson, *Lucy, the Beginnings of Humankind* (New York: Simon & Schuster, 1990).

3. Melvin D. Joesten, John L. Hogg, and Mary E. Castellion, *The World of Chemistry* (Belmont, CA: Thomson Brooks/Cole, 2007), 291.

4. Daniel L. Reger, Scott R. Goode, and David W. Ball, *Chemistry: Principles and Practice* (Belmont, CA: Cengage Learning, 2009).

5. Mike J. Walker, *Quaternary Dating Methods* (West Sussex: John Wiley & Sons, 2005), 3.

6. Garth Wiebe, *The Parable of the Candle,* [Online], available, http://www.answersingenesis.org/articles/1998/05/21/candle-parable (accessed January 7, 2012).

7. Cecie Starr et al., *Biology: The Unity and Diversity of Life* (Belmont, CA: Cengage Learning, 2009), 268.

8. D. C. Creagh and David A. Bradley, *Radiation in Art and Archeometry* (Amsterdam: Elsevier Science B. V., 2000), 256.

9. Deborah A. Slee and Vergil N. Slee, *Slee's Health Care Terms 5th Ed* (Sudbury, MA: Jones and Bartlett, 2008), 46.

10. Peter J. Russell, Paul E. Hertz, and Beverely McMillian, *Biology: The Dynamic Science (Second Edition)* (Belmont, CA: Brooks Cole, 2008), 25.

11. Slee, *Slee's Health Care Terms 5th Ed.*

12. Park S. Nobel, *Physicochemical and Environmental Plant Physiology: 4th Ed* (Burlington, MA: Academic Press, 2009), 410.

13. Mary E. Malainey, *A Consumer's Guide to Archaeological Science: Analytical Techniques* (New York: Springer, 2010).

14. Reed Wicander and James S. Monroe, *Historical Geology: Evolution of Earth and Life Through Time* (Belmont, CA: Cengage Learning, 2009), 77.

15. Malainey, *A Consumer's Guide to Archaeological Science: Analytical Techniques.*

16. Tatjana Jevremovic, *Nuclear Principles in Engineering* (New York: Springer, 2009), 209.

17. John Avison, *The World of Physics* (Cheltenham, UK: Thomas Nelson and Sons, 1989).

18. Ron Shaw, *Great Scientists and Discoveries* (Carlton South Vic, Australia: Curriculum Press, 2003), 61.

19. David J. Cuff and Andrew Goudie, *The Oxford Companion to Global Change* (Oxford: Oxford University Press, 2008).

20. John C. Kotz, Paul Treichel, and John Raymond Townsend, *Chemistry and Chemical Reactivity Vol. 2* (Belmont, CA: Cenage Learning, 2009), 1076.

21. M. S. Baxter and A. Walton, "Fluctuations of Atmospheric Carbon-14 Concentrations during the Past Century," *Proceedings of the Royal Society of London* 321, no. 1544 (January 1971).

22. Wicander and Monroe, *Historical Geology: Evolution of Earth and Life Through Time*, 77.

23. Karl W. Butzer, *Environment and Archeology* (Chicago: Aldine-Atherton, 1971).

24. Nobel, *Physicochemical and Environmental Plant Physiology*, 410.

25. B. S. Chisholm, *The Chemistry of Prehistoric Human Bone* (Cambridge: Cambridge University, 1989).

26. R. Park and S. Epstein, "Carbon Isotope Fractionation during Photosynthesis," *Geochim* 4090750 (December 2009).

27. W. Libby, "Radiocarbon Dating, Memories, and Hopes," *Proceedings of the Eighth International Radiocarbon Dating Conference* 1, no. 721019 (October 1972).

28. D. C. Lowe, "Problems Associated with the Use of Coal as a Source of 14C Free Background Material," *Radiocarbon* 31, no. 2 (1989).

29. Libby, "Radiocarbon Dating, Memories, and Hopes."

30. Jonathan M. Hal, *A History of the Archaic Greek World* (Malden, MA: Blackwell, 2007), 34.

31. Reed Wicander, *The Changing Earth: Exploring Geology and Evolution 5th Edition* (Belmont, CA: Cenage Learning, 2009), 459.

32. Scott Lamoureux, *Tracking Environmental Change Using Lake Sediments; Varve Chronology Techniques* (New York: Kluwer Academic, 2002), 11.

33. Johannes Van Der Plicht, "The Groningen Radiocarbon Calibration Program," *Radiocarbon* 35, no. 1 (1993).

34. Rainer Berger, "Suess,'" *Wiggles and Deviations" Proven by Historical and Archeological Means," SAO/NASA* 20, no. 2 (June 1985): 395.

35. William E. Doolittle, Dendrochronology, http://uts.cc.utexas.edu/~wd/courses/373F/notes/lec20den.html (accessed August 31, 2012).

36. Walker, *Quaternary Dating Methods*, chap. 5.5.

37. Ibid.
38. Don DeYoung, *Thousands Not Billions: Challenging an Icon of Evolution, Questioning the Age of the Earth* (Portland: Master Books, 2005).
39. Ron Edwards and Lisa Dickie, *Diamonds and Gemstones* (New York: Crabtree Publishing Company, 2004).
40. Berger, *Wiggles and Deviations quota; Proven by Historical and Archeological Means, "* SAO/NASA.
41. DeYoung, *Thousands Not Billions: Challenging an Icon of Evolution, Questioning the Age of the Earth.*
42. Ibid.

7. COSMOLOGY

1. Lisa Randall, *Knocking on Heaven's Door* (New York: Harper Collins Publishers, 2011), 10.
2. Eleftherios Papantonopoulos, *The Invisible Universe: Dark Matter and Dark Energy* (Athens, Greece: Springer, 2007).
3. Randall, *Knocking on Heaven's Door.*
4. Arthur Gibson, *God and the Universe* (New Fetter Lane London: Routledge, 2000).
5. Govert Schilling, *Atlas of Astronomical Discoveries* (New York: Springer, 2008).
6. Hans Volker Klapdor-Kleingrothaus, *Dark Matter in Astrophysics and Particle Physics, 1998* (Danvers, MA: IOP Publishing, 1999).
7. Richard F. Kitchener, *The World View of Contemporary Physics: Does It Need a New Metaphysics?* (Albany: State University of New York Press, 1988).
8. Randall, *Knocking on Heaven's Door.*
9. Lisa Randall, Knocking on Heaven's Door: How Physics and Scientific Thinking Illuminate the Universe and the Modern World (New York: Harper Collins, 2011), sec. V., 2011).
10. NASA, *Available.*
11. Ibid.
12. John Gribbin, *In Search of the Big Bang: Quantum Physics and Cosmology* (New York: Bantam Books, 1986).
13. Michael J. Behe, *Darwin's Black Box: The Biochemical Challenge to Evolution* (New York: Simon & Schuster, 1996).
14. National Research Council (US) Committee on the Physics of the Universe, comp. and ed., *Connecting Quarks with the Cosmos: Eleven Science Questions for the New Century* (Washington, DC: National Academic Press, 2003).
15. Simeon Hellerman and Ian Swanson, *Dimension-Changing Exact Solutions of String Theory* (New York: Cornell University, 2006).

16. Mohsen Razavy, *Quantum Theory of Tunneling* (Singapore: World Scientific Publishing, 2003), 4.

17. Kara Rogers, *The 100 Most Influential Scientists of All Time* (New York: Britannica Educational Publishing, 2010).

18. Milton Karl Munitz, *Theories of the Universe: From Babylonian Myth to Modern Science* (New York: Free Press, 1957).

19. Joseph A. Angelo, *Encyclopedia of Space and Astronomy* (New York: Infobase Publishing, 2006).

20. Stephen Hawking, *The Beginning of Time*, [Online], available, http://www.hawking.org.uk/index.php/lectures/62 (accessed December 6, 2011).

21. John E. Chambers, "Planetary Accretion in the Inner Solar System," *Science Direct* (April 2004). And Imke De Pater, Planetary Sciences (Cambridge: Cambridge University Press, 2010).

22. Erik Asphaug, "The Small Planets," *Scientific American* 282 (May 2000).

23. Steven A. Balbus, "A Powerful Local Shear Instability in Weakly Magnetized Disks," *Astrophysical Journal* 376, no. 214 (1991).

24. Avanti Tilak, *Constraints on Jets and Accretion Disks in Low Luminosity Radio Galaxies* (Harvard: Harvard University, 2006).

25. De Pater, *Planetary Sciences*.

26. Peter H. Bodenheimer, *Principles of Star Formation* (New York: Springer, 2011), chap. 4.

27. F. Palla, *Physics of Star Formation in Galaxies* (New York: Springer, 2002).

28. Carole Stott et al., ed., *Space: From Earth to the Edge of the Universe* (New York: DK, 2010), 214.

29. Bo Reipurth, David Jewitt, and Klaus Keil, *Protostars and Planets V, Volume 5* (Tucson: University of Arizona Press, 2007).

30. R. Wayne, Spencer, Can We See Stars Forming?, [Online], available, http://www.answersingenesis.org/articles/aid/v3/n1/star-formation-and-creation (accessed December 7, 2011).

31. [Staff?], comp., Voyager Spacecraft finds Solar System is Bigger than Thought, http://www.cnn.com/2012/12/03/us/space-voyager-solar-system/index.html (accessed December 18, 2012).

32. Kevin B. Marvel, *Astronomy Made Simple* (New York: Broadway Books, 2004), 142.

8. EPIGENETICS

1. Charles Darwin, *The Origin of Species* (New York: Gramercy, 1979).

2. Charles Darwin, *Insectivorous Plants* (New York: D. Appleton and Company, 1875), chap. 3.

3. U. S. Government employees, National Human Genome Research Institute, [Online], available, doi:www.genome.gov/12011239 [accessed September 28, 2011].

4. NOVA, *Available*.

5. Nicole Davis, *Broad Institute Awarded Major Grant to Bolster Epigenomics Research*, [Online], available, www.broadinstitute.org/news/press-releases/1104 [accessed September 14, 2011].

6. Robert Hooke, *Microgrpahia: Or Some Physiological Depictions of Minute Bodies Made by Magnifying Glasses* (London: National Library of Medicine, 1665).

7. Jon Balchin, *Science: 100 Scientists Who Changed the World* (New York: Enchanted Lion Books, 2003).

8. Brian J. Ford, *Advances in Imaging and Electron Physics* (Amsterdam: Academic Press, 2009).

9. Gurbachan S. Miglani, *Developmental Genetics* (New Delhi: I.K. International Publishing House, 2006), 443.

10. Janice Glimm-Lacy and Peter B. Kaufman, *Botany Illustrated: Introduction to Plants, Major Groups, Flowering Plant Families* (New York: Springer, 2006), 7.

11. Jose A. Karam, *Apoptosis in Carcinogenesis and Chemotherapy* (Netherlands: Springer, 2009).

12. David Sadava, Heller Hillis, and Berenbaum, eds., *Life: The Science of Biology 9th Edition* (S, n.d.), land, MA: Sinauer Associates,, 2011), chap. 13..

13. Jan Sapp, *Genesis: Molecular Biology and Organismic Complexity* (Oxford: Oxford University Press, 2003), 188.

14. Ayeda Ayed and Theodore Hup, *Molecular Biology Intelligence Unit* (New York: Springer Science & Business Media, LLC, 2010), chap. 1.

15. J. Bertram, "The Molecular Biology of Cancer," *Molecular Aspects Medicine* 21, no. 6 (2000).

16. Fredrick Hoyle and Nalin Chandra Wickramasinghe, *Astronomical Origins of Life: Steps Towards Panspermia* (Dordrecht, Netherlands: Kluwer Academic Publishers, 2000).

17. Werner Gitt, *The Wonder of Man* (Bielefeld, Germany: Christliche Literatur-Verbreitung, 1999), 65.

ϒ Spetner uses fifty trillion cells for his calculation, a conservative quantity as some estimates go as high as one hundred trillion. No one knows the true amount as there are too many variables such as body size. A large percentage of our cells are bacteria, viruses, and microorganisms.

18. Lee M. Spetner, *Not by Chance* (New York: Judaica Press, 1998), 30.

19. Martin Beckerman, *Molecular and Cellular Signaling* (New York: Springer Science + Business Media, 2005), 22.

20. A. D. Goldberg, C. D. Allis, and E. Bernstein, "Epigenetics: A Landscape Takes Shape," *Cell* 128, no. 4 (February 2007).

21. David C. Allis, Thoms Jenuwein, and Danny Reinberg, *Epigenetics* (Cold Spring Harbor, NY: Cold Spring Harbor Laboratory Press, 2007).

22. Richard C. Francis, *The Ultimate Mystery of Inheritance: Epigenetics* (New York: W. W. Norton & Company, 2011), Preface.

23. Ibid.

24. Ibid., chap. 2.

25. Bruce Stillman, *Epigenetics: Symposia on Quantitative Biology* (Cold Springs Harbor, NY: Cold Springs Harbor Laboratory Press, 2004).

26. M Anthony, *Changing Societies: Essential Sociology for Our Times* (Lanham, MD: Rowman & Littlefield Publishers,, 1999), 118.

27. Jeffrey S. Nevid, *Psychology: Concepts and Applications* (Boston: Houghton Mifflin Company, 2009), chap. 9.

28. Miller, "The Seductive Allure of Behavioral Epigenetics," *Science*, July, 2010.

29. Arthuras Petronis and Jonathan Mill, eds., *Brain, Behavior and Epigenetics* (New York: Springer-, 2011), 75.

30. John Cloud, "Why Your DNA Isn't Your Destiny," Time, *Wednesday*, January 6, 2010.

31. Ibid.

32. Ibid.

33. Mary M. Bauer, *The Truth about You* (Acton, MA: VanderWyk & Burnham, 2006), 87.

34. Ibid.

35. Stan Lee, "Spider-Man," *Columbia Pictures*.

36. Randy Jirtle, *Epigenetics: Environmental Factors Can Alter the Way Our Genes Are Expressed*, NOVA transcript, July 24, (n.p.: NOVA, 2007).

37. Day and Sweatt, *DNA Methylation and Memory Formation*.

38. James Gills, *The Mysterious Epigenome* (2011), 1718.

39. Carl E. Thoresen, "Spirituality and Health: Is There a Relationship," *Journal of Health Psychology* 4, no. 3 (May 1999).

40. Jeremy J Day and J David Sweatt, *DNA Methylation and Memory Formation*, [Online], available, www.nature.com/neuro/journal/v13/n11/full/nn.2666.html [accessed September 16, 2011].

41. Miller, "The Seductive Allure of Behavioral Epigenetics."

9. THE HOW AND WHY OF APOLOGETICS

1. James Strong, *The Exhaustive Concordance of the Bible* (Peabody, MA: Hendrickson Publishing, 1988).

2. Dan Story, *Engaging the Closed Minded: Presenting Your Faith to the Confirmed Unbeliever* (Grand Rapids: Kregel Pub., 1999), 45.

10. SIX LITERAL DAYS

1. Dana Blanton, *Most Believe Prayer Heals*, 45% believe in Creationism, [Online], available: www.foxnews.com/politics/2011/09/07/fox-news-poll-most-believe-prayer-heals-45-believe-in-creationism/?test=latestnews [accessed September 8, 2011].

2. Eugenie C. Scott, "The Creation/Evolution Continuum," *Reports of the National Center for Science*.

3. G. Bouw, "A Response to de Young's Ex Nihilo Article," *Bulletin of the Tychonian Society* 53 (1990).

4. Stephen J. Gould, *Rock of Ages* (NY: Ballantine Publishing Group, 1999).

5. Richard Dawkins, *The God Delusion* (New York: First Mariner Books, 2006).

6. Douglas Potter, *Response as Primary Reader to This Ministry Project* (Matthews, NC: Southern Evangelical Seminary, 2012).

7. Herbert W. Armstrong, *Mystery of the Ages* (New York: Mead, 1985).

8. Hugh Ross and Gleason Archer, *The G3n3s1s Debate* (Mission Viejo, CA: Cruxpress, 2001).

9. John C. Whitcomb, "Progressive Creationism," *Impact*, no. 360 (June 2003).

10. Stephen C. Meyer, "The Origin of Biological Information and the Higher Taxonomic Categories," *Proceedings of the Biological Society of Washington* 117, no. 2 (2004).

11. Casey Laskin, Intelligent Design and the Origin of Biological Information: A Response to Dennis Venema, *Available*.

12. Michael J. Behe, *Darwin's Black Box* (New York: Free Press, 1996).

13. William A. Dembski, *Intelligent Design* (Downers Grove, IL: InterVaristy Press, 1999).

14. Gonzalez Guillermo, *The Privileged Planet* (Washington, DC: Regency Publishing, 2004).

15. Peter Jedicke, *SETI: The Search for Alien Intelligence* (North Mankato, MN: Byron Press Visual Publications, 2003).

16. Melanie Phillips, *The World Turned Upside Down: Global Battle Over God, Truth, and Power* (New York: Encounter Books, 2010), 74.

17. P. H. Rampelotto, "Panspermia: A Promising Field of Research," *The Smithsonian/NASA Astrophysics Data System*, no. 1538 (April 2010): 5224.

18. John McArthur, *John McArthur Study Bible* (Nashville: Thomas Nelson, 1997), 16.

19. Rampelotto, "Panspermia: A Promising Field of Research, 5224.

20. Gleason L. Archer, *Encyclopedia of Bible Difficulties* (Grand Rapids: Baker, 1982).

21. Norman L. Geisler, *Baker Encyclopedia of Christian Apologetics* (Grand Rapids: Zondervan, 1999), 271.

22. Archer, *Encyclopedia of Bible Difficulties.*

23. Barry Leventhal, *Class Discussion* (Matthews, NC: Southern Evangelical Seminary, January 6, 2012).

24. Ken Ham, Jonathan Sarfati, and Carl Wieland, *Did God Really Take Six Days?* (Green Forest, AR: Masters Books, 2006), chap. 2.

25. Hugh Ross, *A Matter of Days: Resolving a Creation Controversy* (Colorado Springs: NavPress, 2004).

11. A FINAL THOUGHT

1. Douglas Kelly, Philip B. Rollinson, and Frederick T. Marsh, *The Westminster Shorter Catechism in Modern English* (n.p.: Presbyterian and Reformed Pub., 1986).